ghostdancing

Deepak Verma

All the best, Naresh,

Sameena

Methuen Drama

Methuen

1 3 5 7 9 10 8 6 4 2

Published in Great Britain in 2001 by
Methuen Publishing Limited,
215 Vauxhall Bridge Road,
London SW1V 1EJ

Copyright © 2001 Deepak Verma

The author has asserted his moral rights

Methuen Publishing Limited Reg. No. 3543167

A CIP catalogue record for this book is available from the British
Library

ISBN 0 413 77179 2

Typeset by SX Composing DTP, Rayleigh, Essex
Printed and bound in Great Britain by
Cox & Wyman Ltd, Reading, Berkshire

Caution
All rights in this play are strictly reserved and application
for performance, etc., should be made to Tamasha
Theatre Company, Unit E, 11 Ronalds Road, London
N5 1XJ. No performance may be given unless a licence
has been obtained.

Tamasha Theatre Company
in association with
the Leicester Haymarket Theatre
present:

ghostdancing

Written by Deepak Verma
Based on Emile Zola's novel *Thérèse Raquin*

First performance of this production,
Wednesday 8th October 2001

ghostdancing

will tour to the following venues:

Week beginning:

8th October 2001	Lyric Theatre, Hammersmith
5th November 2001	Leicester Haymarket Theatre
13th/14th November 2001	Contact Theatre, Manchester
16th/17th November 2001	Alhambra Theatre, Bradford
19th November 2001	Gulbenkian Studio, Newcastle Playhouse
26th November 2001	Bristol Old Vic
3rd December 2001	Gadesjakket Teatret, Copenhagen

ghostdancing

Written by Deepak Verma

cast
(in order of appearance)

Raj	Shammi Aulakh
Rani	Anjali Jay
Leila	Sameena Zehra
Doctor	Simon Nagra
Nitin	Rehan Sheikh

production

Director	Kristine Landon-Smith
Designer	Sue Mayes
Lighting Designers	Chris Davey
	and Tim Bray
Composer	Felix Cross
Movement Director	Lawrence Evans
Production Manager	Tom Albu
Company Stage Manager	John Blunden
Deputy Stage Manager	Debbie Hunt
Costume Supervisor	Nujma Yousef
Animation Advisor	Manju Gregory

Set built and painted by
Leicester Haymarket Theatre Workshop

Paintings by Rebecca Whitehead

Tamasha wishes to thank Nicky Jones, Nitro
and Kathy Bourne

The Company

Shammi Aulakh (Raj)
Shammi was classically trained at the London Academy of performing Arts. His many and varied credits include, *Bina's Choice* (Dominion Centre), *Survivors* (Orange Tree Theatre) and Tamasha's *Balti Kings* and *Fourteen Songs, Two Weddings and a Funeral*. His work in commercials includes the role of an Indian Father (Hindi and English versions) on the Kodak World Wide Moments campaign. Most recently Shammi filmed a role in the upcoming movie *Doctor Sleep* for Kismet Films with Goran Biznik of the hit American hospital drama series *ER*.

Sudha Bhuchar (Artistic Director)
Sudha is co-founder of Tamasha Theatre Company. She is both an actor and a playwright. Her many acting credits include *EastEnders* (BBC), *The Archers* (BBC Radio) and *Haroun and the Sea of Stories* (Royal National Theatre). Her writing credits for Tamasha include *Untouchable*, *A Tainted Dawn* and *Balti Kings*. She also writes regularly with Shaheen Khan for BBC Radio 4, this autumn will see their screenplay, *The House Across the Street*, debut on BBC 4.

Tim Bray (Lighting Designer)
Following a residency as Deputy Chief Electrician at the Lyric Theatre Hammersmith, Tim left to pursue more opportunities in lighting design. His credits include *The Arabian Nights* (Marlowe Theatre in Canterbury), *The Dreaming* (National Youth Music Theatre), *The Deep Blue Sea* (Nottingham Playhouse) and *The Knack* (ENO work). He has also designed for a promenade performance and installation at Hoxton Hall, London and St Pancras. This is his second show with Tamasha, having previously assisted Chris Davey on *Balti Kings*.

Felix Cross (Composer)
Felix Cross has been the Artistic Director of NITRO (formerly Black Theatre Co-operative) since 1996. He recently wrote the book, music and lyrics for *Passports to the Promised Land* for NITRO. Other work includes *Blues for Railton* (Albany Empire), *Glory!* (Temba/Derby Playhouse), *Mass Carib* (Albany Empire/South Bank) and *Integration Octet* (for string quartet and steel pan quartet at Aldeburgh Festival/ Royal Festival Hall). He wrote the music and lyrics to *Jekyll & Hyde* and *The Bottle Imp* (both books by Graham Devlin, Major Road). With Paulette Randall he wrote the book for *Up Against the Wall* (Black Theatre Co-op). He regularly composes for Radio 4 dramas and has also written the music for over fifty stage plays, most recently, the entire canon of Agatha Christie's plays, for the Palace Theatre Westcliff.

Chris Davey (Lighting Designer)

Chris's theatre designs include *The Three Sisters* (Oxford Stage Company), *Shining Souls* (Peter Hall Season at the Old Vic), *In a Little World of Our Own* and *Endgame* (DonmarWarehouse), *The Colour of Justice* (Tricycle Theatre) and *Balti Kings* (Tamasha Theatre Company). Dance theatre credits include, *Transatlantic Tap* (Dance Umbrella) and *Turn of the Tide* (Shobana Jeyasingh Dance Company). Opera credits include *Gli Equivoci Nel Sembiante* (Batignano Opera Festival), *The Picture of Dorian Gray* (Opera de Monte Carlo) and *Faust* (Surrey Opera).

Lawrence Evans (Movement Director)

Lawrence works as a movement director, director and actor. He was nominated for an Olivier award for Choreography for his work at the Royal National Theatre. He has also worked with the poet and playwright Tony Harrison on all of his site-specific theatre pieces since 1988, touring to Greece, Austria, Denmark and Bradford. He is an associate artist of Theatre Centre Professional Theatre for Young People and his play *Lives Worth Living* is published by Heinemann.

Anjali Jay (Rani)

After graduating with an MA from The Laban Centre of Movement and Dance, Anjali worked ostensibly for Shobana Jeyasingh Dance Company. Theatre credits include *A Ramayan Odyssey* (Riverside Studios), *Genesis* (Tara Arts) and she played Scheherazade in *Arabian Nights* (Oxford Touring Theatre). She has appeared in many commercials and has undertaken various radio roles for the BBC.

Kristine Landon-Smith (Director)

Kristine is joint founder and Artistic Director of Tamasha and has also directed all of the company's shows. Other companies she has worked with include the Royal Court Theatre, Hull Truck Company and she has been an Associate Director of the Bristol Old Vic. Her 1996 production, *East is East*, was nominated for an Olivier award and the original production of *Fourteen Songs, Two Weddings and A Funeral* won the Barclays Theatre Award for Best New Musical. Kristine produces regularly for BBC radio.

Sue Mayes (Designer)

Sue has designed all of Tamasha's shows. Her career started with residencies at Ipswich Rep, the Belgrade Theatre and the Liverpool Everyman. Her other freelance work has included designs for Talawa Theatre Company, Bristol Old Vic, Theatre Royal Stratford East and the Southwark Playhouse.

Simon Nagra (Doctor)

Simon's recent theatre productions include *Arabian Nights* (Duke's Playhouse Theatre, Lancaster), *Crime of the 21st Century* a new play by Edward Bond (UK tour and Croatia), *Play to Win* (Soho Theatre, London and tour), Salman Rushdie's *Haroun and the Sea of Stories* (National Theatre), *Cultivated Wilderness* (Spectacle Theatre), *A Song for a Sanctuary* (Lyric theatre, Hammersmith), *Kahinni* (Birmingham Rep) and Asaph Chawn in *Aureng-Zebe* (National Studio). On television he has been seen in *The Bill* and *EastEnders*. His radio credits include *Saving Grace*, *Hillcrest* and *A New Life*.

Rehan Sheikh (Nitin)

Rehan is a well-known television actor and presenter in Pakistan, having successfully combined a career both here and there for the past seven years. His credits in Pakistan include *Dozuka*, *Bisaat*, *The Castle*, *Awaazain* and *Kiran Kahani*. Other work includes *Ragni* for Rafi Peer International Theatre Festival (Lahore) and *Ek Admi* (One man at Camden's People's Theatre). He has also done extensive work for the radio and has written three plays (performed at fringe venues), one short film and a feature length tele-film. This will be Rehan's sixth production for Tamasha, having most recently appeared in *Fourteen Songs, Two Weddings and A Funeral*.

Deepak Verma (Writer)

Deepak Verma is best known for his portrayal of Sanjay, in BBC TV's *EastEnders*, which he left in 1998. Since leaving, he has set up his own film and television production company, Pukkanasha Films and is currently producing and will be starring in a feature film *Johnny Bollywood*, a romantic comedy. He is also developing a slate of projects with various companies including the BBC and is currently working on his next stage play and first screenplay.

Sameena Zehra (Leila)

Sameena has a degree in psychology and literature. Born in India, she has been living in the UK now for five years where a large part of her work concentrates on using role-playing for theatre in training to promote an understanding of equal opportunities issues. This is Sameena's third show with Tamasha, having previously played the roles of both Kamla and Bhagwanti in *Fourteen Songs, Two Weddings and A Funeral*.

tamasha

Tamasha is one of Britain's leading theatre companies on the national touring circuit. We provide a unique experience of theatre, with stories drawn from the Asian community both in Britain and the Indian sub-continent. Our work traverses beyond the Asian community and is accessible to a growing culturally diverse audience. From adaptations of literature to new commissions, Tamasha has a firm commitment to nurture and produce the work of British Asian writers.

Tamasha was formed in 1989 by Kristine Landon-Smith and Sudha Bhuchar to adapt *Untouchable*, a classic Indian novel by Mulk Raj Anand. Over the past twelve years, the company has produced nine plays, five of which have been adapted for Radio Four and two of which have won the CRE Race in the Media Awards. Their 1997 production, *East is East* transferred to the West End and has since been made into a highly successful film.

Tamasha is funded by the Arts Council of England, London Arts and the London Borough Grants scheme. The company has collaborated with prestigious producing houses including Birmingham Repertory Theatre, the Lyric Theatre Hammersmith, the Royal Court Theatre, the Bristol Old Vic and the Theatre Royal Stratford East.

Artistic Directors	Kristine Landon-Smith
	& Sudha Bhuchar
General Manager	Bryan Savery
Administrator	Claire Gossop
Development Officer	Joe Moran
Head of Marketing and PR	Suman Bhuchar
Marketing Assistant	Harpreet Kaur
Outreach Marketing Co-ordinator	Ruby Sangha
Education Consultant	Sita Brahmachari
Press Consultant	Ben Chamberlain
Marketing Consultant	Mark Slaughter
Production Photographer	Charlie Carter

Tamasha Theatre Company
Unit E, 11 Ronalds Road, London, N5 1XJ
T: 020-7609 2411   F: 020-7609 2722
E: info@tamasha.org.uk   www.tamasha.org.uk

Registered charity number: 1001483

tamasha's past productions

1989 **Untouchable**
Adaptation by Sudha Bhuchar and Kristine Landon-Smith,
from the novel by Mulk Raj Anand.
If UNTOUCHABLE *is the fruit of their first efforts, Tamasha seems
set to lead the way in the ensuing decade —* TIMES OF INDIA

1991 **House of the Sun**
Adaptation by Sudha Bhuchar and Kristine Landon-Smith,
from the novel by Meira Chand.
*Not just one for the Asian community, but a warm, witty comedy
of city life —* TIME OUT

1993 **Women of the Dust**
Written by Ruth Carter
*Sue Maye's sun baked setting creates a tremendous sense of place
on the Riverside's panoramic stage and Kristine Landon-Smith's
production is powerfully played —* EVENING STANDARD

1994 **A Shaft of Sunlight**
Written by Abhijat Joshi
*This play was quite simply, one of the most mesmerising and absorbing
80 minutes I have ever spent in a theatre —* REDDITCH OBSERVER

1995 **A Yearning**
Adaptation by Ruth Carter from the novel *Yerma* by Lorca
*A thought-provoking production, opening a surprisingly accurate
window into the aims and aspirations of the Punjabi community in our
own city —* BIRMINGHAM WEEKLY OBSERVER

1996–7 **East is East**
Written by Ayub Khan-Din
A delightful new comedy…Kristine Landon-Smith's immensely attractive production – THE INDEPENDENT

1997 **A Tainted Dawn**
Written by Kristine Landon-Smith and Sudha Bhuchar
I doubt if any theatre company anywhere will bring the disappointment and disillusion of 1947 so grittily to life… – THE TIMES

1998–2001 **Fourteen Songs, Two Weddings And A Funeral**
Adapted from the Bollywood film *Hum Aapke Hain Koun..!*
by Kristine Landon-Smith and Sudha Bhuchar
(FOURTEEN SONGS, TWO WEDDINGS AND A FUNERAL) *has a naïve charm and melodic gaiety that puts most london musicals in the shade* – GUARDIAN

2000 **Balti Kings**
Written by Sudha Bhuchar and Shaheen Khan
Will linger in the memory for a long time, like the dramatic equivalent of really good curry – DAILY TELEGRAPH

The Leicester Haymarket Theatre is one of the country's leading producing theatres, and is especially renowned for its musicals. The Theatre presents around 500 performances each year in a wide-ranging programme of musicals, classic and new plays, Asian theatre, children's theatre, international drama and dance, community and educational events. The Leicester Haymarket Theatre is also known for its pioneering and ground breaking Asian theatre work. The company has adopted a policy of Integrated Theatre whereby all strands of its work will be threaded together through the joint artistic direction of Paul Kerryson and Kully Thiarai. Together they bring a new way of working and sharing theatre to Leicester, Leicestershire, the region and the nation.

The Leicester Haymarket Theatre also hosts visiting companies such as Shared Experience, Paines Plough, The Reduced Indian Film Company, Tamasha Theatre Company and Siobhan Davies Dance Company.

Shows created, nurtured and developed in Leicester have been seen throughout Britain and the world. These include *Hamlet*, *Julius Caesar*, *M. Butterfly*, *The Queen and I* and *Disappeared*. The success of the Leicester Haymarket Theatres musical productions has led to many of them transferring to the West End including *My Fair Lady*, *High Society*, *Me and My Girl*, *Hot Stuff* and *Mack and Mabel*.

The Leicester Haymarket Theatre has gained an enviable reputation for its exciting and adventurous programme of work and, above all, for the quality of its productions.

Chief Executive: Mandy Stewart

Artistic Directors: Paul Kerryson & Kully Thiarai

Broadway's out, Leicester's in. — SUNDAY TIMES

Staged at the pioneering venue Haymarket Theatre in Leicester the play has all the ingredients that made the film a success — ASIAN TIMES, East is East

Now and then a show, a production, a performance, reminds me why I fell in love with the theatre. Paul Kerryson's production of Sondheim's enchanting musical has done just that. Perfection — THE TIMES, A Little Night Music

Leicester Haymarket Theatre, Belgrave Gate, Leicester LE1 3YQ

Box Office 0116 253 9797

e-mail enquiry@leicesterhaymarkettheatre.org

www.leicesterhaymarkettheatre.org

Registered charity no. 23070

Lyric Theatre Hammersmith

Welcome to the Lyric Theatre Hammersmith.

Hidden away behind a concrete facade on a busy high street, this is one of the most surprising theatres in London. We use it to put on our own shows, and also to make work with a range of award-winning companies from Tamasha to the Royal Shakespeare Company, to host exciting newcomers like Frantic Assembly, The Right Size and Improbable Theatre Company.

When we put on a show, we want to reach as wide an audience as possible. Our education and community programmes, together with our ticket prices, make sure that the doors to the Lyric are open to everyone, in Hammersmith, West London, and beyond.

I hope you enjoy tonight's show, *Fourteen Songs, Two Weddings and a Funeral* and I hope you come back to the Lyric again.

Neil Bartlett, *Artistic Director*

Executive Director
Simon Mellor

Artistic Associates
Tim Albery
Rachel Clare
Michael Morris

Next at the Lyric:

Lyric Theatre Hammersmith & Forkbeard Fantasy presents
Frankenstein - A truly Monstrous Experiment, 7-24 November

Lyric Theatre Hammersmith & Told by An Idiot presents
Aladdin - An Arabian Night Out, 30 November - 12 January

Information & Tickets: 020 8741 2311
email : boxoffice@lyric.co.uk
Web : www.lyric.co.uk

Lyric Theatre Hammersmith is a Registered Charity No. 27851

ghostdancing

Act One

Scene One

Rani *comes into the room carrying* **Raj**. *She puts him down on the sofa.* **Raj** *is coughing violently. His fit gets gradually stronger.*

Raj   Rani! Get me some water. Anybody would think I'm a cripple. This filthy city has done this to me. Give me the salts! All I see is dirt and grime . . . and when I am at work, nothing but the smell of oil . . .

Rani *gives him water and gets a bag of inhaling salts. He sniffs them.*

Raj   This won't do anything to me. That Doctor says that there is nothing wrong with me. These blasted hakim types – witch doctors. Let me put my head on your lap – bring the medicine . . .

Rani *makes to go. He stops her.*

Not yet – in a while . . .

Rani *sits on the couch and* **Raj** *lies down with his head on her lap.*

Raj   Where is Mother? Mother!

Rani   Downstairs. The shop is busy. That new khuder is selling very well – winter comes and all the cotton goes.

Raj   Just stroke me . . .

Rani *strokes* **Raj**'s *head. She seems in a world of her own.*

Raj   You know the railways these days are a disaster. They employ the Gunandwalas to arrange the railway lines and they can't get their wallets out to fix the electric cabling. Whenever I meet anybody that I know on the street they always torment me: 'You work with the railways,' they say, 'get them to arrange things better.' Damn people . . . (*Coughing.*) I am a clerk . . . only . . . a paper checker . . . (**Raj** *starts coughing again.*)

Rani   Do you need more water?

Raj   Get the medicine – quickly! I won't get any rest without it . . .

He starts to breathe slowly and with difficulty. He is in great pain.
Rani *goes to get the medicine out of a nearby cabinet.*

Raj   It's Thursday – you know we have guests coming. Did you get spinach? And the cornflour . . . ?

Rani   Everything is ready. Mother has already started to prepare the dinner.

Rani   Here. (*She hands him the medicine.*)

Raj   Will you drink some as well?

Rani *is clearly used to this request. She drinks the medicine.*

Raj   Just to make me feel better. Now, give it to me . . .

Rani *puts some medicine into a glass and feeds it to* **Raj**.

Raj   I want to have fun tonight. All this doom and gloom, hey!

Leila *enters.*

Leila   What were you shouting about?

Raj   We have a special visitor coming tonight.

Leila   Who? The Doctor?

Raj   No. He's always here. No – somebody else. You will see. But don't start your . . . you know . . .

Leila   What? You think I am mad?

Raj   We have an important person coming. He thinks that I too am a man of some note. So having my mother talk to me like I am a child, somehow tarnishes my reputation . . .

Leila (*hurt*)   You are not the only one with a mother . . .

Raj (*holding her close*)   Mother – it's all right. I suppose I will have to surrender to another night of shame and embarrassment.

Leila   So – who is it? The special guest . . . ?

Raj   You will see. I feel weak mother. Why am I being tortured so much? The medicine that your friend gave me does nothing . . .

Leila   Raj – don't ignore the Doctor's advice. Now – the mustard leaves are ready and the maki ki roti . . . But Rani, my dear, you must learn not to make the bread so tough. You have to be careful to turn it in time, otherwise it isn't maki ki roti . . .

Rani   Yes, Mother.

Raj   You have been teaching her since your brother left her with you – seventeen years. How long does it take? Blasted head is aching . . . will it never end?

Rani *starts massaging* **Raj**'s *head, almost automatically.*

Leila   You have been working too hard my child. Life is not all about work. I have done nothing but give you medicines since you were born.

Raj   You know that Choudhary boy? That greasy-haired one with the bumfluff moustache? Hardly out of his mother's lap? They have given him the post of Deputy! Unbelievable! There am I, working hard, good background . . . No doubt he is the illegitimate son of one of the directors or something . . .

He starts coughing again.

Leila   Don't fret about other people's success. God gives everybody his share – just be patient.

Raj   How can they promote somebody who still suckles his mother's breast?

Leila   Raj – have you no shame?

Raj   The boy is only nineteen – all right? Anyway, I command respect from a lot of people. It's amazing how a uniform can change the way people look at you. Now, make sure everything is ready. My special friend will be here soon. Shall we eat first or . . . ?

Leila   Well, we will see what your friend and the Doctor want to do.

Raj   The Doctor just wants to play karom all night and tell tall stories. But tonight is not his night . . .

Leila   He is an important person. Years ago he used to come and help me when I had the shop in the village. When your father died there was nothing that he wouldn't do for me. He loved your father – now I look upon him as a brother . . .

Raj   I never understood why he is called a doctor. He is a hakim – a homeopathic doctor. Degrees can be bought in bazaars these days . . . for a few rupees. He says that he studied in England. I don't believe him. I can see through his affected accent.

He laughs and **Rani** *shares a smile with him.*

Leila   Raj! I don't want you being stupid tonight. Now, here is the karom board. If that is what the Doctor wants, then I shall be happy to see him enjoy himself in this house. A guest is a gift from God . . .

Raj *starts breathing heavily again. A knocking.*

Raj   He's here! He's here!

Doctor (*off*)   Leila!

Raj   Oh – it's only the Doctor . . .

Leila *goes to let the* **Doctor** *in.* **Raj** *controls his breathing and gulps down a glass of water. He stands up as the* **Doctor** *enters.*

Raj   Evening, Doctor. Oh Mother – you didn't listen to the story the Doctor told us last time – about the village girl? Remember, Doctor? Tell me now. Oh yes – it was quite fascinating . . .

Leila   Give the Doctor a chance to settle down first. He's hardly put his foot in the door . . .

Doctor   He is teasing. He fell asleep when I was speaking.

Raj   No, honestly Doctor . . .

*The **Doctor** is clearly used to talking this audience through his experiences and he starts telling the story as if he was there in person.*

Doctor   The village girl . . . oooh, yes! Yes. Her husband was very unhappy with her. There was talk of her having a male friend somewhere. I realised that the pains in her stomach were because she was full of baby. I told the husband and his family to leave me alone with her. They were adamant that she was possessed and had demons in her that had to be beaten out. I took her to one side and told her to admit that she was possessed. I took her by the neck and squeezed hard – there are two points, which, when pressurised, can manipulate movement in various parts of your body . . .

*He demonstrates this on **Raj**.*

Her arms started flailing . . . I gave her an injection and took a huge pan full of boiling water, threw various herbs into it and then held her head close to an inch of it. I then took a metallic rod with spikes and beat her. The fact was, that if I hadn't done this whilst protecting her honour, somebody less understanding might have destroyed her forever. She fainted. I took her inside for half an hour, where I cleansed her of her misdemeanour. I then proclaimed her clean of bad spirits. I still see her when I go to the village. She has two children now . . .

Raj   Amazing . . .

Leila   Many a filthy thing happens in a village.

Raj   I misjudged you all these years, Doctor. Not only are you a hakim, you are also a psychologist with a bit of community concern thrown in . . .

Doctor   There is nothing wrong with you at all. You are as fit as a horse. Leila – you shouldn't mollycoddle him so much. But it's too late now. You know nothing more than the warmth of the armpit of your mother . . .

There is a loud knocking.

Raj   Mother – the door . . . it's my . . . guest. I'll get him . . .

Raj *rushes down.*

Leila   Don't be too hard on him, Mohan. He is a bit fragile at the moment.

Doctor   He needs to learn to be a man.

Raj   Come up, Nitin. Come on my boy – don't be shy . . .

Enter **Raj** *followed by a smartly dressed* **Nitin**. *A very good-looking man in his mid-twenties.*

Raj   Do you recognise him?

Leila   No . . .

Nitin   I bought some sweetmeats.

Leila   Raj has been teasing me about you . . .

Raj   Look carefully at him, Mother – don't you know him?

Leila   Stop this game, Raj. Introduce us properly.

Raj   Nitin – this is my mother, the good Doctor – a close friend of the family – and my wife, Rani. Nitin's dad owned the cornfields near Moga and we went to school together. You used to give us tiffin boxes sometimes.

Leila   Ahhh! And your uncle lived near us. Yes – now I remember. But if you will change your name, how can I keep up?

Nitin   Yes, I was known as Babloo . . .

Leila   Just look at you – a fine hunk of a man! Come and give me a hug. Babloo . . . yes. You liked the paronthas with potatoes . . .

Raj   He used to steal mine sometimes. He works at the same place as I do. Eighteen months we've been working for the Railway and I only met him a few weeks ago . . . imagine! It proves how important the Railway is and the size of it! He has a degree. His father has been good to him – hasn't he, Nitin?

Nitin   Yes. I have to say that . . .

Raj   And he also paints – isn't that the truth? Portraits, with his own perspective on the person. He takes a particular idiosyncrasy from the person's face and exaggerates it . . .

Nitin   Well – yes, that is one of the things that I can do – caricatures. But straight portraiture is something that fascinates me as well . . .

Leila   Rani – get our guest a drink and some food.

Nitin   I am not very hungry yet – I'll wait.

Leila   We'll all have some tea. Just look at you Babloo . . . *(She pinches his cheek.)* You've still got those lovely dimples . . . Babloo . . . Rani – come and help me. (**Leila** *exits.*)

Raj   Rani, wait! Nitin – you remember my wife, don't you? *(Sharing a joke with himself.)* Ahhh! Now it's your turn to play guessing games. Recognise her? Think back to the village . . . and our house . . .

Nitin   Ahhh . . . wait . . . ahhh, yes. Your cousin – the little girl . . . of course . . .

Raj   Yes – the one who I teased you about being your future wife! Ahhh! Now you know . . .

Nitin   Raniji – how are you? You look very healthy and . . . happy . . .

Rani   Yes – we are doing very well . . .

Raj   We have a cloth shop downstairs. We sell all sorts of materials – from the most expensive silk, to everyday cotton . . .

Rani   I'll get the tea . . .

Leila (*off*)   Doctor Sahib! Come and help me open this sack!

Doctor   Ahhh!

He rushes off.

Raj   How is your father?

Nitin   For five years we have been strangers. He wanted me to be a lawyer. You said that I had a degree? Well, I don't. I merely pretended to study law – went to a few lectures. My old man was sending me a good allowance, but when he realised that I was not interested in law he dried me up. I was living with a friend who was an artist and when I tried my hand at the easel, I found my aim in life. The job at the Railway offices just helps to fund my painting. The old man is sick and he is sure to die soon – so I am waiting for the time when I can live and not have to work.

Raj   What great bohemianship! Fantastic! So – you are waiting for your father to die and leave you lots of money? Enabling you to . . . meander without aim. The man's a genius!

Nitin   If a man doesn't have an obsession, then what is the point in him being alive? I live for art . . .

Raj   Ahhh – liar . . . liar. I know that in actual fact, what you want to do and what your body wants to do, is – nothing!

Nitin   Perhaps. To sink in never-ending idleness and to indulge myself. After all, that is what God wants man to do.

I might become a guru and have my wicked way with lots of females . . .

This entertains **Raj**, *who starts to laugh.*

Raj   Did you paint . . . you know – as is the tradition? Nudes?

Nitin   Oh – when I think about it I realise how much I miss Angad's studio. We had an exciting time there . . .

Raj   Did women take their clothes off for you to paint them?

Nitin   All the time. Then we took them for a hot cha afterwards – there were a lot of foreigners there.

Rani *walks in with a tray of food / tea.* **Nitin** *and* **Raj** *are unaware of her presence.*

Raj *(excited)*   So tell me about the models . . .

Nitin   I had one – absolutely stunning . . . Her hair was like fire – long . . . flowing . . .

Raj   Yes?

Nitin   Her body was firm – she told me she enjoyed swimming – and it showed in her sinews. Her breasts were as firm as melons and as big as her head . . . and she . . .

He sees **Rani**, *who stares at him with intensity and he tries quickly to finish the sentence.*

Nitin   And . . . Uhh . . . I . . . well . . . Just . . . and I painted her quite often.

Raj   Foreign women . . . the thought is beyond . . . *(Notices* **Rani**.*)* Ahhhh – Rani!

Rani   Tea.

Leila *enters.*

Leila   Come on, Rani – lay the table.

Raj   Where is the Doctor?

Leila   He hurt his back lifting a bag of onions. I am destined to be surrounded by weaklings! Now we have a real man in the house – Nitin. Everybody . . . Yes . . . Nitin is a bull of a man and look at those big hands! And what a thick, short, well-built neck he has. Don't you think Rani?

Rani *is too embarrassed to say anything. She starts serving.*

Leila   Have you done much work in the fields?

Nitin   Not really – that bores me. But I have a friend who has a few horses, so I ride them.

Leila   Raj does no exercise. I keep telling him, but . . .

Raj   Mother – please!

Leila   I am just saying that a bit of exercise can do . . .

Raj   Did you know, Mother, that Nitin paints? Draws pictures . . .

Nitin   I must paint you, Raj – what do you think?

Raj   Yes! Oooohh! Yes – isn't that exciting? To have a real painter paint me? Only the high flyers do that . . . oooooh! Rani – tea for Nitin.

Rani *pours tea for* **Nitin** *and puts it in front of him.*

Nitin   It's all right, I'll . . .

Raj   Here – pakoras. Come on, Rani. Are you not going to look after our guest?

He grabs a handful of pakoras and throws them on to **Nitin**'*s plate.*

Nitin   Uhhh . . . thank you.

The **Doctor** *comes struggling up.*

Doctor   Ahhh – damn blasted back! Ahhh . . . all I did was bend a little bit. Hi Bhagwan!! That's it – I've pulled something . . .

Raj   No, Doctor, no. It's psychosomatic. There is no pain there really – it's all in your head . . .

Leila   Don't tease, Raj . . .

Nitin   Sit down, Doctor.

The **Doctor** *sits on a chair.* **Nitin** *starts to touch his shoulders and neck.* **Rani** *studies* **Nitin** *with intensity.*

Nitin   I am just getting to feel what your muscles are doing. As a painter, you get to know the human body very well . . .

Doctor   Ohh . . .

Nitin   Lift your head from the back as if a rope is pulling you from here. Now – I have noticed that the way you stand is very slouched. So all the effort is being taken by your lower back – here . . .

Doctor   Ahhhh!

Nitin   Now – I am just going to . . . push your shoulders out. Stand up . . .

The **Doctor** *does so.*

Nitin   Now . . .

He pushes the lower back.

Nitin   And . . .

He pulls it hard.

Doctor   Ow! Ahh! . . . Oh I see . . . that's what you were doing . . . Now I was going to suggest that . . . but . . . Yes I feel taller . . . Yes it feels much better. The man is an expert!

Raj   Nitin is going to paint me! Oh – but Nitin – I want a stylish portrait. Not those pictures where you paint my nose like an aubergine . . .

Nitin   All right – a straight portrait. But I have to warn you that it will take a bit of time to get it right. And you have to sit still for hours . . .

Raj   Not a problem, Nitin. In fact, I have made a skill out of sitting still – at work that is all I do . . .

Leila   Where are you living, Nitin?

Nitin   Just a small room in the D'Souza Marg.

Leila   That's a terrible street!

Nitin   Only if you are part of what goes on there . . .

Raj   D'Souza Street. How very high-class.

Leila   High-class prostitutes, maybe . . .

Raj   Mother, you have to keep up with the times. D'Souza Marg is an up-and-coming area.

Leila   The houses there are mere mouseholes.

Nitin   For a single man on his own, a small place is the best thing. You don't have to worry about cleaning up. I just spend as much time as I can outside and go to the room as late as possible.

Leila   But that's not healthy, Nitin. Where you live is very important.

Nitin   I take my easel outside and because the weather is fine these days, one can paint sitting on the pavement . . .

Leila   Well – you are welcome here any time you want. There is a spare room – open invitation for dinner any night you want . . .

She exits to the kitchen.

Raj   He'll have to come now – as he is going to make a masterpiece of my face . . .

Nitin (*he stares at* **Rani**)   Maybe I should paint your wife first?

Raj   Why?

Nitin   She has a natural beauty . . . and a translucent feel to the skin. Sorry, Raniji – I was talking like an artist . . . I didn't mean to be so forward . . .

Rani   You are forgiven. (*She laughs.*)

Raj   Ha! Yes, you should paint her – after you have finished with me. And I'll take the painting in to my work . . . show them all . . . show them that Raj is a man worthy of having his portrait painted! (*He laughs.*)

Scene Two .

Nitin *is finishing painting* **Raj**. **Rani** *is watching with great interest.*

Nitin   Now, it's been your left eye that has given me a problem. I want to get that slight line as accurately as possible. It represents the weakness of man and the transience of life. We are all doomed to die. That is the one guarantee in life – death. Keep still, Raj. You have a beautiful wife. What ills a man would suffer to have the privilege of such a woman sharing one's life – what reason to complain Rajoo Bhai?

Rani (*embarrassed*)   I am going down to help Mother . . .

Nitin   Actually, would you help me to finish this work? The painting is complete – just a few more strokes and I think, Raj, you will be happy . . .

Rani   What do you want me to do?

Nitin   To shower your blessing on this work. I feel that it is endowed with a truth which at first is difficult to grasp, but eventually the person who looks at it will decipher the actuality of things.

Raj   Are you sure it is not a – what did you call it – a caricature?

Nitin   No. It's most definitely not a caricature. Raniji –
please . . .

He signals for her to come near him. She hesitates.

Raj   Go on, Rani. The master has summoned you.

Nitin   Now, look . . .

Rani *studies the painting.*

Nitin   You see the eyebrow? It needs a few more strokes
and the portrait is finished.

Rani   Yes.

Nitin   What is your first response?

Rani   It is very dark – the background is very dark . . .

Nitin   Shall we finish it? Please take this brush . . . and just
finely go over the . . . eyebrow . . .

Rani *pauses.*

Rani   No – I'll ruin it . . .

Nitin   Let me . . .

He comes behind her and guides her arm on the easel.

Nitin   Slowly. I can see the purity flooding into the
painting already . . . Now let's just fill in that little gap . . .
and . . . finished!

Raj   Mother! It's finished! Mother – come up!

Rani   I can see what you mean about the truth.

Nitin   You can see? I'm glad – it makes things much
easier . . .

Raj   I will hold my curiosity for a while longer – we should
celebrate.

Leila *enters.*

Leila   So, it's finished – after all these hard evenings . . .

Raj   Rani – get the bottle of brandy. What a joyous occasion! Now can I take a peek?

Nitin   Let me unveil it to you when everybody is here. Bhabi helped me to finish it.

Leila   I didn't know she could paint.

Raj   She merely flicked a few lines on . . .

Rani *brings the brandy.*

Nitin   No, Raj. The picture is now endowed with the greatest thing we have – the energy of a woman . . . the beauty of a woman . . . It is a tradition of mine to have a female hand wander over my work. Now, ready . . .

He turns the painting towards **Raj** *and* **Leila**. *A pause.*

Raj   I look ill.

Nitin   But brother, you are ill. You were saying just now . . . But it has a touch of . . .

Raj   My cheeks are concave . . .

Nitin   The truth is the truth . . .

Leila   It's lovely. Very good. Babloo has worked very hard – coming here every evening and going home late . . .

Rani   It's an achievement. You can see the truth . . . Yes . . .

Nitin   Rajoo – it makes you look bohemian. Look, the hair – it's a bit longer in the picture because I thought it makes you look like a poet – a tortured soul . . .

Raj   How exciting . . . really?

Leila   Is everybody hungry? Food is ready.

Scene Three

Evening, a few days later. **Rani** *is on her own. She is staring at the painting. She touches it. A loud knocking.*

Nitin (*off*) Hello?

Rani Who is that?

Nitin It's Nitin . . .

Rani Oh!

She rushes out. She returns with **Nitin**.

Nitin For a moment I thought that you weren't going to let me in. Why is it closed downstairs? The shop usually closes at five . . .

Rani Mother and Raj have gone to the next town to pick up new stock.

Nitin Oh. Well, I brought some brandy for Raj and some sweetmeats for Mother . . .

Rani That's very kind. They'll be a few hours yet. They left me to close the shop . . .

Nitin (*he indicates the brandy*) Would you allow me to offer you a drink?

Rani Me? (*She laughs.*)

Nitin Why not?

Rani I don't know any women who drink.

Nitin Why is it wrong for a woman to do what men spend their entire life doing?

Rani It's what some women are used to.

Nitin Are you happy?

Rani What do you mean?

Nitin That is the simplest question one human can ask another. Are you content? I see a sadness in your eyes. To me it's clear – you are in despair . . .

Rani I am very happy and Mother has given her whole life to bringing me up and giving me all that I need . . .

Nitin No. No. No! You are not happy in the least. Is anybody happy when it comes down to it? We all live in a world of broken dreams – some of us die without ever having dreamt at all. The ability to dream is not instilled in all of us. Do you dream?

Rani I dream . . . yes . . .

Nitin You are a very lucky woman. You have a saint of a mother-in-law. You have a dedicated husband. Taking that as fact, it is easy for us to distance ourselves and really explore the depths of our minds. Tell me about your dreams – are you sure that you don't want a drink?

Rani I dream about the sea – I would love to see the sea again . . .

There is an awkward atmosphere between them, but **Nitin** *grows increasingly confident.*

Nitin The sea?

Rani Yes – the sea would be enough. Perhaps you should go . . . I mean . . . Isn't it improper for us to talk like this?

Nitin Why? I am talking to you like a brother . . .

Rani As a brother?

Nitin Of course. Is the sea your only dream?

Rani What is *your* dream?

Nitin To settle down perhaps, at some point. Women of today are far too . . . manly. They go around acting like men – they cut their hair like men, they wear trousers . . .

Rani   City girls – giving all the rest of us a bad reputation . . .

Nitin   They make men feel impotent. So – what else do you long for? What is your dream? (*He gets closer to her as he is asking the question.*)

Rani   I have all that I require . . .

Nitin   Then you are a very lucky woman indeed. Do you think they'll be long?

Rani   Who?

Nitin   Mother and Raj.

Rani   Oh, they'll be a couple of hours yet – the road is very long to Ludhiana . . . and narrow . . . and they went by truck . . .

Nitin   Well – I'll go. You're probably getting bored of all this. I apologise, but it is one of my hobbies – digging into the soul. Did you know that I was once a saint?

Rani   A saint?

Nitin   It's all humbug! Anybody can grow a beard, read a few Upanishads . . . and bang! You are a saint! Then watch them fall at your feet. I was in the hands of a guru – a teacher – I learnt the art of Not Knowing. And the freeing of the souls. From him I received the key to unlock the cage of my preconceptions. He showed me the dance of the free spirit – the act of unlocking. He showed me how to Ghostdance. Our bodies are the manifestation of our soul. If the body is free, then the soul shall also be free. It's a difficult thing, but once you master it, you become the master of your soul, and of your destiny . . .

Rani   (*completely entranced by his words*)   Is it something that you can teach?

Nitin   You mean – for instance if you wanted to learn?

Rani   I want to be free. I want . . . sorry . . . please go!

Nitin   Go on. Be brave – tell me . . .

Rani   I am suffocating . . . drowning . . . in an abyss of time. The same . . . day in and day out . . . There is no world out there – I am a slave to my circumstances . . .

Nitin   Did you choose to do what you are doing at the moment? Did you choose any of it?

Rani   It's what I know. What I have been taught . . .

Nitin   Taught by whom? Ask yourself that. And who benefits? The answer is in your soul. You can take control – by actively seeking what you desire. Your being has atrophied . . . bring it back to life. Choose to live. Choose . . .

Nitin *looks at her closely. He touches her cheek. She starts to sob.* **Nitin** *goes closer to her. He holds her hand. He grabs her violently. They kiss. She resists.* **Nitin** *goes to kiss her again, but* **Rani** *slaps him and starts to beat him with her fists, harder and harder.* **Nitin** *backs off. She approaches him as if attacking prey. A violent embrace.*

Blackout.

Act Two

Scene One

Six months later. **Rani**'s *bedroom.*

The embrace is almost the same as we left it. **Rani** *is screaming.*

Nitin   Shhhh! You want the old woman to come up?

Rani   She won't – she's far too busy making money . . .

Nitin   She'll be wondering where you are . . .

Rani   What is wrong with you – are you a man?

Nitin   Do you want the whole street to know what we are up to?

Rani   I don't care if they do – I don't care! I love you . . .

Rani *approaches him. He backs off.*

Nitin   You look like a madwoman when you do that . . .

Rani   You didn't know how mad when you took advantage of me six months ago . . .

Nitin   YOU took advantage of me! Anyway it was written on your face that you needed to take a lover . . .

Rani   Years of bowing and yessing. And now – if they only knew . . . All of us gathered together on a Thursday evening – the Doctor playing karom with Raj . . . and us exchanging glances – stealing a touch here and a grope there – I couldn't feel better. Do I look better?

Nitin   Your face is flushed with the vibrancy of life . . .

Rani   This – my revenge. For all that they have put me through. Look – come here. Look through the window – see that monkey?

Nitin   Yes – it's always there, isn't it?

Rani   I call him Hanuman after the monkey king. Imagine if he could talk? He would tell everybody about us, wouldn't he? He would go into the shop and say: 'The artist man sneaks through the side entrance, which leads straight to the bedroom and embraces her. I have never seen Mr Raj do that with her. I put it to you that they are both guilty. And how loud she is . . . '

Nitin   I think there is somebody coming . . .

Rani   No – she won't leave the shop . . .

Nitin   Shhhh! Listen . . .

Rani   No. No . . . Yes! It's her . . .

Nitin *quickly grabs his clothes.*

Nitin   You idiot! I told you not to make any noise . . .

Rani   Get in the bed . . .

Nitin   I'll go . . .

Rani   No – she'll see you.

She pushes him into the bed.

Rani   Keep quiet!

She throws her clothes on to the bed, and gets in. **Nitin** *is hidden.*
Leila *opens the door.*

Leila   What is the matter?

Rani   Just tired . . . and I have a little headache. Nothing more. Get back to the shop Mother . . .

Leila   I locked it for a while – it's very quiet . . .

Rani   No – you must stay there. If they see it's locked they'll just walk past. I'll be down soon.

Leila   There is a lot of work to be done. After all, the Doctor and Nitin are coming tonight . . .

Rani   I don't like Nitin. He is always eating and drinking at our house and acts as if he owns the place.

Leila   Rani beti – don't speak about Raj's friends like that. Nitin is a good boy and has made our life very exciting. Painting and telling us stories . . .

Rani   Mother, please don't worry about me – attend the shop . . .

Leila   Why don't you keep this room tidy? Clothes strewn all over the place . . . Clean up before Raj comes back.

Rani   Yes.

Rani *turns to sleep.* **Leila** *goes.* **Rani** *waits a minute. Silence. She bursts out laughing.* **Nitin** *peeks a look and looks silly with her petticoat on his head.*

Scene Two

At the table. The **Doctor** *and* **Raj** *are playing karom.* **Rani** *is sewing. The painting of* **Raj** *is prominently displayed on a wall.*

Raj   Where the devil is Nitin? He's a very bad timekeeper. Mother was saying that you don't like him, Rani . . .

Rani   I just think he takes advantage of us . . .

Raj   I like him. Don't you think Nitin is an amiable kind of fellow?

Leila *comes in, having heard all this. She carries food and drink.*

Leila   He is a poor creature all alone in the world.

Doctor   Yes – Nitin is lost in a world of his own. Just like me . . .

Leila   How are you these days, Doctor?

Doctor   Well. Yes – it's going very well indeed. You see I have had an eye on a female for some time. And slowly I am getting closer to her . . .

Leila   You devil, Doctor . . .

Doctor   In answer to your question – I am very well. But alas the world is full of malady. What strange things go on. And you don't know the very people around you. Who they are and what they are thinking . . . conniving . . . plotting. It's frightening indeed . . .

Raj   Come on, Doctor. What's happened?

Doctor   Let's continue with the game.

Raj   I refuse to play. You can't do that – you must tell me . . .

Doctor   Do you know that woman who lives three streets away? The young one with gold teeth? Mara?

Leila   Mara – the Yehudi . . .

Doctor   Yes.

Leila   She has a rich husband somewhere. They say that although she is the owner of many properties, she won't move from her small flat.

Doctor   Yes. Is she a nice woman? Do you know her?

Leila   I've only met her a few times. She came into the shop to buy three huge rolls of white cotton. Said she was making curtains for one of her properties.

Doctor   My God . . .

Leila   What is it?

Doctor   You sold her white cotton – normal cotton?

Leila   Not the cheapest . . . middle range . . .

Raj   What are you 'Oh Godding' for, Doctor?

Doctor   Have you passed her house recently?

Raj   What a good storyteller you are – spinning out the story. What about Mara?

A knocking.

Raj   Damn knocking . . .

Leila   Raj – it's probably Nitin. Why have you started cursing so much recently?

She goes out.

Rani   He's come to eat our food again.

Raj *suddenly turns to* **Rani**. *He slaps her.*

Raj   How dare you speak out like that? I am the man of the house and will do exactly what I want!

Doctor (*trying to maintain a normal atmosphere*)   Yours, young fellow. Are we playing or not?

Raj   Yes – a woman should never speak against a man. Isn't that right?

Nitin   Raj, Doctor . . .

Raj *gets up and makes a point of hugging him.*

Raj   We were wondering where you were. What kept you?

Nitin   You know what I'm like – strolling, looking around, examining the very space around me to see if there is anything worth committing to the canvas . . .

Raj   And was there anything?

Nitin   I can't tell you. You might steal my ideas.

Raj   Why is everybody having difficulty telling me anything tonight? Doctor, will you finish your story?

Doctor   Hey?

Raj   About the Yehudi woman – Mara? What was the point?

Doctor   She is dead.

Gasps of surprise.

Leila Dead?

Nitin What's happened?

Raj One of the Doctor's long, drawn-out stories. Dead is she? How – what happened?

Doctor Can you guess how?

Raj She was sick, wasn't she? In fact, wasn't she one of your patients?

Doctor Yes – that's just it . . . exactly! They say she was murdered . . .

Raj Murdered? Killed?

Doctor I was only there a few days ago. She mentioned that her ex-husband had suddenly appeared out of nowhere a few days before and asked her to deny her claim to his fortune.

Raj You know him?

Doctor Not really.

Raj Doctor – will you spit it out? Now – now . . .

Doctor Yes, I know him – not very well. He is also a sick man. But Mara made his life hell. And as you know, Leila – what they said about Mara . . .

Leila Yes.

Raj What?

Rani Will you stop wittering on like a child – 'what-whatting'? Can't you talk like an adult?

A stunned silence.

Raj What did you say?

Nitin (*laughing, trying to make good the situation*) Stop teasing him, Bhabi . . .

Raj How dare she insult me in front of . . .

Nitin   It's not an insult . . .

Leila   She's ill. She's been in bed the whole afternoon.
Poor child . . .

Nitin   It's all right. Now, Bhabi I really feel like some tea.
Would you . . . get me some?

Rani *looks at* **Raj**.

Raj   Yes – go on. If you are sick, then rest.

Rani   I had a headache before. I'm all right now – just . . .
weary. I'll get the tea.

Doctor   Would you like me to take a look at her, Rajoo?

Raj   No. No . . .

Nitin   Have you been looking after her? My Bhabi needs a
lot of attention . . .

Doctor   You never know, Raj. There may be a good
reason why she is like this. Maybe she's . . .

Raj   No. Nothing of the sort. Now, where were we? Ah –
so what was it that they say – said about Mara?

Leila   She had gentlemen callers . . .

Raj   What, her? But she was old . . .

Leila   So were the gentlemen callers . . .

Raj   How was she killed?

Leila   Can't we talk about pleasant things?

Raj (*ignoring her*)   How was Mara killed?

Doctor   We are about to eat. Let's try and keep the
conversation less unsavoury. She was chopped up into little
bits. Now, let's continue with karom. I will thrash you,
young sir . . .

Raj   Chopped? Isn't that exciting? Right down the street from us – our very own murder! Did you tell anybody that she told you about her husband visiting her?

Doctor   Why should I?

Raj   It's a clue – isn't it? A special clue . . . Doctor, you are involved in an intrigue. Why did you show huge surprise when Mother told you that she bought cotton from us?

Doctor   The fact is that her parts were wrapped in cotton . . .

Leila   Hi Bhagwan!

He starts to cough.

Raj   Water, Mother . . .

Nitin   It's all right Mother, I'll get it . . .

He goes out. **Raj** *continues spluttering.*

Leila   Such a sweet boy. Did you hear that? He called me Mother . . .

Raj   It's getting worse, Doctor. The pain in my chest is like a knife being twisted in my flesh.

Doctor   What you need is fresh air – the mountains. That will get you up and about. I bet you don't listen to me about herbs and vegetables? Ayurvedic – that is the future, Raj – everything ayurvedic. The ancient form of life . . .

Raj   I tried it, Doctor. It tasted like mud . . .

The scene continues as **Nitin** *and* **Rani** *share an embrace in the kitchen. The focus is split between the kitchen and* **Rani**'s *room.* **Nitin** *fondles* **Rani**. *She screams.*

Raj   What's the matter Nitin?

Nitin   Nothing, Raj. Just molesting your wife . . .

Raj   Good man. Bring the water will you? Cold as possible. He's funny, isn't he?

Shift focus to kitchen, where **Nitin** *is making love to* **Rani**. **Nitin** *is holding her.*

Rani   Take me away from this! The whole world should know that I'm your woman . . .

Nitin   Can't you see? What we have is perfect . . .

Rani   Don't you long for more?

Nitin   Yes – but everything has its time.

Rani   This is the right time. We are strong together. I want you, Nitin. Now, make the next move – take the next step . . .

Nitin   I can't . . .

Rani   What?

Nitin   I can't afford to. I barely get by on my wages alone. And I need time for my art . . .

Rani   Your art?

Nitin   Why are you behaving like this?

Rani   We have been together like man and wife for six months. Raj hasn't touched me for over a year. Am I strange in wanting more?

Nitin   No . . .

Rani   Why don't we let them find us together? Then they'll throw me out . . .

Nitin   And then what?

Rani   I'll stay with you.

Nitin   That would be difficult . . .

Rani   You mean, you can't look after me?

Nitin   It's not the right time – trust me. Look – today I was called up by my boss, I've taken too many afternoons

off to see you and it has . . . my boss wants me to increase
my workload and work beside him, as his assistant . . .

Rani   Can't you get another job?

Nitin   My life will be a mess if I lose that job. I am
incapable of working.

Rani   You'll just walk away when you please, leaving me
tortured and confused and worse off than I was – stuck in
this nightmare . . .

Nitin   I won't be able to meet you in the afternoons, that's
all. I'll still come over in the evenings . . .

Rani   Why don't we let them watch whilst we're at it? Go
– leave me alone!

Nitin   Stop it . . .

He goes nearer. He touches her face.

Nitin   Let me think . . . Let me think . . .

Rani   Get out!

She slaps him.

Nitin   I love you.

Rani   You love yourself – son of a pig!

Nitin *maintains his composure.*

Rani   You're just a selfish oaf!

Nitin *starts laughing.*

Nitin   Stop being so childish. You look silly like that. Your
face goes red and your nose looks like a bhangan.

Rani   You think it's funny? Go – you've hurt me enough.
I don't want to see you again.

Nitin *goes.* **Rani** *is left. Her new lease of life has gone.*

Nitin *comes back to the gathering with water.*

Nitin   Here.

Raj   Hey, Nitin, the Doctor thinks I should go away . . .

Nitin   Great idea, yaar . . . Yes.

Raj   You think I should?

Nitin   Of course. We'll look after Mother and Bhabi.

Doctor   No, dear boy. I think she should go with him. And I shall look after Leila . . .

Nitin   Oh – of course. Yes . . . good . . . Where were you thinking?

Raj   I don't know . . . Kullu Valley, you said?

Doctor   Yes.

Leila   I heard there was a bus that fell from the mountain in the Kullu Valley.

Doctor   Let him go with his wife and relax. It will help him enormously – and put him on an ayurvedic diet . . .

Raj   Mother will think about it. Shall we continue the game?

Nitin   Will you two hurry up? I want to play the Doctor at karom and show him what's what . . .

Doctor   Now there is a challenge . . .

Scene Three

Two weeks later. **Nitin**'s *flat. He is staring at a letter. The clock strikes seven.* **Nitin** *sighs. He paces around. Knocking.* **Nitin** *opens the door.* **Rani** *wearing a coat.*

Nitin   I couldn't believe that you were coming . . .

Rani   I told them that I was collecting payments that were owed to the shop. I can't stay long.

Nitin *grabs her. He kisses her.*

Nitin   I'm sorry – I was stupid. It's taken all this time apart from you for me to see that I want you. It's torture seeing you at the house. Not being able to touch you. I have a hunger that I didn't know about . . .

He picks her up. She wraps her legs around him. They slip to the floor and make love, raw and animal-like.

Nitin   When will you come again?

Rani   Never. How can I make excuses to go out of the house?

Nitin   But I need to see you . . .

Rani   We can't.

Nitin   Your husband is a disease – a pain in my soul. Why don't you just get rid of him? Tell him to go away . . .

Rani   I don't drink his medicines any more.

Nitin   I want to spend the whole night with you and wake up in your arms. Is that what you want?

Rani   Yes!

Nitin   Come and see me tomorrow.

Rani   I can't – it's not possible . . .

Nitin   I do want to be yours. Your husband and protector . . .

Rani   Yes? Why didn't you say that the last time we met?

Nitin   Everything happens when it's meant to. We should be careful . . .

Rani   Why?

Nitin   It's for the best. You don't want to ruin my reputation, do you? You care about me – yes?

Rani   I love you.

Nitin   I'll keep away from the house and the shop. It will
be difficult, but . . . Oh! If only he were to die . . . die. That
would solve everything . . .

Rani   Yes – we could do what we want then. People do
die. But it's the people that are left behind that are hurt –
wounded. She would be heartbroken. But he won't die.
Have you got some money? I can say that I cleared the
debt . . .

Nitin   I'm broke this week. I get paid in a few days.

Rani   I'm going now . . .

She makes to go.

Nitin   I don't know when we will see each other.
Remember me, will you?

Rani   Yes.

She rushes out. **Nitin** *studies the postcoital scene. He could almost be
crying. He picks up the blanket which earlier had wrapped* **Rani***, and
smells her presence. He starts to pace around.*

Scene Four

Raj*'s house.* **Doctor***,* **Leila***,* **Rani** *and* **Raj***. The usual
gathering.*

Raj   I have been a fool – an idiot! I have realised that
moaning and groaning about aches is the worst thing for
me. It makes me worse . . .

Doctor   If you start telling your body that you are well,
then you shall be well.

Raj   And I am – I am! And I am important – aren't I,
Mother?

Doctor   Told you! There was nothing wrong with him.
He needed to start telling himself that he is fit.

Leila   Of course. *(She embraces him.)* You are the most important thing in the world to me. And you and Rani are here to look after me – aren't you?

Raj   Yes. Rani – look after mother. Massage her feet.

Rani *doesn't move.*

Raj   Massage Mother's feet . . .

Rani *begrudgingly starts rubbing* **Leila***'s feet. Knocking.*

Raj   Who is that?

Rani   I'll answer it. *(She rushes off.)*

The doorway. **Nitin** *stands there looking distraught.*

Rani   What's the matter? You look like a ghost . . .

Nitin   I want you to be my wife. Without you I am a dead man . . .

She kisses him and fondles him. They enter the lounge. **Rani** *is still and quiet through this scene. There is an atmosphere of discomfort between* **Nitin** *and* **Rani***. They share glances throughout the scene.*

Raj   Nitin, my friend – you've been avoiding us . . .

Nitin   Rajoo. Mother. Doctorji.

Nitin *is feigning exuberance and energy.*

Nitin   I've been busy. *(He laughs.)* You know what us artists are like. I was concentrating on a new work . . . I needed time for myself . . . to study life . . .

Doctor   Yes. Life. What an extraordinary thing. Do you know, there were further developments in the whole Mara episode?

Raj   The Jewish woman?

Doctor   Yes. They found her husband under her floorboards!

Raj   But I thought he was the main suspect?

Doctor   Yes. But obviously there are other hands involved. There was talk of a particular lover. They say that he was so infatuated with her, that he took it upon himself to erase the estranged husband who was making her life difficult. They've had people around there all day – strolling in and out of the house like a zoo. Poor Mara . . . People have no respect when a spectacle is to be made out of human misery. And they say that this lover has disappeared abroad somewhere . . .

Raj   Nitin, you know that they have given me more duties at work? They even gave me a new coat! I want to show you, Nitin. Wait!

He rushes out, giggling with excitement. The **Doctor** *starts laughing.*

Leila   What's the matter?

Doctor   Nothing. I'm happy . . . to see you all so . . . happy . . .

Raj *enters wearing a ridiculous coat.*

Raj   Isn't it marvellous? What do you think, Nitin?

Nitin   What a fabulous coat! Very distinguished . . .

Doctor   So, as you have a larger salary, you shall have to treat us. Buy us all a present . . .

Raj   They haven't increased the salary yet . . .

Doctor   So they make you work harder, but pay you the same?

Raj   You know what these important institutions are like . . . We shall have to frequent certain gatherings, Mother and Rani. Perhaps we should invite the Head of the Railways – Mirchandani – for dinner? My boss's boss. What do you think, Nitin? Then maybe I'll get promoted . . .

Nitin (*absently*)   Why not?

Leila   We are surely very humble compared to these people. Why would he come to a small house such as ours?

Raj Utter nonsense, Mother. We are very well-to-do. We have a shop, we have a house with lots of rooms and my beautiful wife – she'll dress up for me. Do you think I should have something done to my hair? It's all the fashion these days to have curls. . .

Leila No, Raj. Your hair is fine. I am not having you looking like a fop. A hijra . . .

Raj Mother, we must keep up with the world. Appearance is very important. Nitin, do you think I should have curls put into my hair?

Nitin I should think curls would suit you down to the ground. And, you know that putting powder on your face is all the rage these days?

Raj Powder?

Nitin I hate using the words, but – 'make-up'. Many men use it . . .

Raj Do you?

Nitin All bohemians use make-up.

Doctor What does that say?

Raj Where?

Doctor On the arm?

Raj Nothing – just the maker's mark.

Doctor No – '*Gandecha*' – that's what it says . . .

Raj Gandecha . . .

Doctor They've given you somebody's old coat, to give you the impression that you are important and they'll work you off your feet . . .

Leila No, Doctor. It's the maker's mark . . .

Doctor Of course it is. So you won't be going away then? As you are feeling better?

Raj No, Doctor – no, no, no! On the contrary – I *shall* be going away, precisely because I *am* better. Kullu Valley, you said?

Leila Rani – get some tea ready. It's been too long since we've seen Nitin . . .

Rani *goes off.*

Raj Now I have an idea – why don't we all go to the hills? Rani and myself, Mother, Doctorji and Nitin? Why not?

Nitin Some of us have to work.

Raj Not at the weekends, Nitin . . . and guess what?

Nitin What?

Raj Looking at my calender I happened to spy that Diwali is on Saturday this year – next week. Why don't we celebrate the festival of lights in Kullu Valley?

Rani *returns with tea and sweetmeats.*

Nitin Are you sure you can handle the journey?

Doctor Of course he can handle it. He is as fit as a monkey.

Raj Yes. Mother – will you come?

Leila Why do you want to drag an old woman with you?

Raj Who says you are old? You are all so boring – we can have a fabulous time there . . .

Nitin Kullu Valley . . . yes, there will be lots to do there . . . and lots of boats . . . We'll all go boating!

Leila No! No boats. Raj is afraid of the water.

Raj No I'm not!

Leila You are. Only Bhagwan and I know how difficult it was for me to wash you when you were a little one. Rani had to chase you around. Isn't it funny to think that you as cousins were brought up together and now you are together as man and wife . . .

Raj   Yes. I am lucky. She's beautiful – aren't you Rani? So, what do you think Doctor?

Doctor   I don't know if I can take it . . .

Raj   But it was your idea.

Doctor   Yes – for you to go, not for me. I am an old man . . .

Raj   Well, why don't you oldies stay here then? Boring!

Nitin   No – we must take Mother and the Doctor . . .

Raj   . . . to celebrate with fireworks! And we'll have lots of good food – it's exactly what I need.

Leila   These hotels are quite expensive though . . .

Raj   No – we have money and I will pay for everything.

Nitin   Are you sure?

Raj   Yes – why can't I treat everybody?

Nitin   We must ask Bhabi. Will you go?

Raj   Of course she'll go . . .

Nitin   Bhabi?

Rani   Whatever you want, Raj.

Nitin   I will be with the people that I love the most in the world: Bhabi . . . and Rajoo.

He embraces the two, one with each arm.

Scene Five

The following week. Kullu Valley. A park. Evening. The cacophony of a distant band, and the occasional firework goes off. **Raj** (*with curly hair and make up*), **Nitin** *and* **Rani** *are lazing.*

Raj   The air is magnificent! Is your room all right, Nitin?

Nitin   Fine – all I need now is a woman to fill it . . .

Raj   Do you think the Doctor loves my mother?

Nitin   Of course. Everybody loves Mother.

Raj   I mean – in a . . . you know . . . romantic kind of way?

Nitin   Maybe he does. Brandy?

Raj   Yes, I will. Why doesn't he just say so then? Let the whole world know . . .

Nitin *pours brandy for* **Raj**. *He doesn't take any himself.*

Rani   Yes. Let the whole world know that he loves a woman.

Raj   He's too reserved. He doesn't seem like the kind of man who could love . . .

Nitin   What rubbish! Of course he can love.

Raj   Nevertheless, I wish he could just say it out loud. Aren't you having any brandy?

Nitin   No – I've had heartburn after the trip. Perhaps later – amidst the Diwali celebrations . . .

Raj   Good. (*He snoozes.*)

Nitin *looks at him. He looks at* **Rani**.

Nitin   Raj . . .

He walks nearer to him.

Nitin   Raj – are you asleep? It's just that I have an idea for you to make lots of money . . .

Raj *doesn't stir.*

Rani   He's asleep. He won't get up for hours, especially after all that brandy you've given him . . .

Nitin   Shhhh!

He moves close to her. He touches her legs. He looks at **Raj** *who is now snoring with his mouth wide open.* **Nitin** *moves closer to* **Raj**. *Whilst moving he caresses* **Rani***'s breasts, out of bravado.*

Nitin (*whispering*)   Shall I do it now?

He picks up a nearby log and walks right in front of **Raj***'s face. He is about to put his heel right in his throat. A stifled moan from* **Rani**. **Nitin** *weighs up his target.* **Rani** *walks away, as if to shield herself from the blood. He stares at* **Raj**.*Walks away.*

Nitin   Look at the flowing water. Where does it come from? A proper mountain stream . . .

Rani   Free. The stream is free to do what it wants . . .

Nitin (*whispering*)   Not like this . . . too dangerous . . . they'll find us. There is a way . . .

Rani   Is there?

Nitin *holds a handkerchief to* **Raj***'s nose.* **Raj** *gets up, sneezing.*

Raj   What? You buffoon! What a way to wake me up! But I'm still tired . . .

Nitin   We have Diwali to celebrate – Raam came home from exile today. Don't you want to celebrate that?

Raj   Yes.

Nitin   Then do it my boy! Open your mouth!

Raj *opens his mouth wide as* **Nitin** *pours the contents of the brandy bottle into it.* **Raj**, *very tipsy, starts playing with a couple of sparklers.*

Rani *watches. It's as if* **Nitin** *and* **Rani** *are playing games with* **Raj**.

Raj   Scoundrel! Lufunga – that's what you are . . . you artist type! Hah!

Nitin   Yes. You're right . . .

Raj   What is this? Sparklers are for children. I want to see bigger fireworks . . .

Nitin   We will. They start later . . .

Raj   Have you ever thought of going away?

Nitin   Yes – I want to go to Europe, to America, everywhere . . .

Raj   I would like to go away somewhere far . . . far . . .

Nitin   How long would you go for?

Raj   Forever. Yes. Somewhere new, where I wouldn't have to return from . . .

Rani   A place from where you never return . . .

Nitin   I'm hungry. Aren't you, Bhabi?

Rani   Yes.

Nitin   Rajoo . . .

Raj   Hungry to experience life . . .

Nitin   Let's go. But wait. Look – boats . . . on the river . . . and look at the fireworks above. Doesn't that look amazing?

Rani   Yes.

Nitin   Why don't we go for a ride, Raj? The boat is ready.

Raj   But Rani is hungry . . .

Rani   Don't worry about me. You go . . .

Nitin   Why don't you order, Bhabi? Go to that one with the red sign above it – the Earl Gray Hotel. We'll see you in there. You can see us from there . . . in the boat. Go!

Rani *goes to* **Raj** *and gives him a hug.*

Rani   Enjoy yourself.

Raj   Yes.

Rani   Be careful. (*She goes.*)

Nitin   I will. Order us some chicken – Kullu Valley chicken is known to be the best . . . Well, Bhai. (*He picks him up.*) We are going on the boat!

Raj   Yes – put me down, Nitin. Put me down.

Rani *re-enters.*

Rani   Can I come with you?

Raj   Yes – let her come . . .

Nitin   Of course. I'm not sure if Raj is feeling confident. Come on, Bhai – help me . . .

They drag a boat out from the bushes. They push it into the water and jump in. **Rani**, *trembling, slowly eases herself in.*

Raj   Nothing scares me now. See, Nitin?

He suddenly throws his arms around him.

Raj   You know I love you, Nitin. Love you. Like a brother . . .

Nitin   I love you, Rajoo.

Loud fireworks going off. Bang! **Nitin** *rows a couple of times and lets the boat float.*

Raj   Bloody narrow boat, yaar!

Nitin   Don't move about too much, otherwise we'll all end up in the water. All right, Bhabi?

Rani   Yes . . .

Nitin   Please just move that way to get the balance right.
Shall we sing a song? I learnt a Gujerati song the other
day . . .

He sings and claps – 'Tume ek waar Marwar Jajo re Oh
Marwara' . . . *etc.* **Raj** *joins in the chorus.*

Raj   '*Oh Marwara*' . . . How far out are we, do you think?

Nitin   Very far out. Are you scared?

Raj   Why should I be, with an expert like you at the helm?
It's much quieter out here . . .

Nitin   Except for the Diwali banging . . .

Raj   Here. This is for you, Nitin.

He gives him a small box from his pocket.

Nitin   What is it?

Raj   Diwali sweetmeats – Diwali mubarak!

Nitin   Diwali mubarak!

Raj   This is the best Diwali I've ever had – except Mother
isn't here . . .

Raj *looks into the water and dips his hands in.*

Raj   It's freezing! I wouldn't want to swim in that!

Rani   The river seems empty now. No boats. No people.
Nothing.

Nitin *gets up and grabs* **Raj** *around the waist.*

Raj   Stop acting the fool, Nitin . . .

Nitin *grabs* **Raj** *around the throat.* **Nitin** *is seized with anger at*
Raj*.*

Raj   What are you doing?

Nitin *tightens his grip on* **Raj***'s throat.*

Raj   No . . .

Raj *sinks into the boat, trying to escape somehow. He is squealing like a dog.*

Raj   No! Help me, Rani – Rani!

Rani   No . . .

She grabs onto the side of the boat and hides like a frightened animal.

Raj   Help!

Rani   No . . .

She weeps. The struggle continues. **Nitin**'*s hold is strong on* **Raj**. *As his hold loosens briefly,* **Raj** *attacks him like an animal.* **Raj** *bites his neck, taking a chunk of flesh off.* **Nitin** *tries to throw him off, but* **Raj** *is strong.* **Nitin**, *with all the strength left in him, throws* **Raj** *out of the boat into the water.* **Raj** *is heard screaming. The screams become weaker and weaker. The screams stop.* **Rani** *is trying to shield herself from the fight. She is in a heap, crying.*

Nitin   Get up . . .

Rani   What have you done?

Nitin   We did it together. Now get up . . .

But she doesn't. He picks her up and shakes her.

Nitin   We've got to think fast. Look – there's a boat approaching. We have to jump in . . . as if our boat has capsized. I'll hold you, don't worry, come on . . .

They jump in. Screams.

Blackout.

Act Three

Scene One

A year later. Diwali night. The sound of fireworks and singing. **Leila**
*is finishing off praying to the shrine which is situated in a corner of the
room. She finishes the prayers and sits in a chair, sobbing. The*
Doctor *soothes her.* **Raj**'s *pathetic face in the picture looks over
them. The picture has garlands around it.* **Rani** *walks in. She is in a
world of her own. She sees something that scares her. Suddenly* **Raj**'s
figure walks past.

Rani (*to herself*)   No! Leave me alone. I don't want to have
anything more to do with you . . . corpse.

*She starts shaking and screams as her body is vibrating. Her movements
are as if she is being taken by a man. A knocking at the door.* **Leila**
stares at **Rani** *in pity for moment and rushes to get the door. She
brings* **Nitin** *in.* **Nitin** *offers* **Leila** *and the* **Doctor** *a box of
sweetmeats. He sees* **Rani** *in the midst of her fit.*

Nitin   Diwali sweetmeats. And for you, Doctor?

Leila   How can we celebrate? I only remember Raj . . .

Doctor   No, Leila. The mourning has got to stop.
Please . . . (*He embraces* **Nitin**.) Diwali mubarak!

Nitin   How is Bhabi?

Leila   Not well. She is saying strange things . . .

Doctor   Leave her. She is hallucinating – talking
nonsense . . .

Leila   Beti – the Doctor is here . . . and Nitin. Will you
greet them?

Rani   Go. Leave me to dance with ghosts . . .

Leila   What's she talking about? Rani – beti . . .

Rani   Silence for the old woman.

Leila *goes to her and holds* **Rani**'s *face.*

Leila   What is the matter? You never speak to me . . .

Raj *walks past.* **Rani** *screams in terror.* **Nitin** *sees him as well. He shudders.*

Rani   I just . . . like the silence in my mind.

Leila *takes her in her arms and holds her.*

Leila   Try not to be sad little one. You know that we are going to start having guests again on Thursdays, just like before . . .

Nitin   She just needs rest, I think. A year ago exactly today. It's bound to have an effect.

He stares at **Rani**, *smiling, as if he wants her to back him up.*

Rani   Yes. Brother is right. It's nothing . . .

Nitin   You must help Mother cope. She needs you – she needs us all . . .

Rani   You want me to forget Raj – erase him from my memory? For me to go to the dances . . . celebrate my widowhood? Tell everybody that Rani is now a piece of unwanted flesh?

Leila   No, Rani. Don't talk like that . . .

Rani   Shall I burn myself? Should I have done that when we were seeing his corpse being touched by the flames? Should I have jumped in and made an end to it?

Leila   Rani – please . . .

Rani   Why not speak the truth? I am sorry . . . I feel sick . . .

She retches and runs off.

Doctor (*under his breath*)   Why don't we just get on with living? This is affecting my karom evenings greatly.

Leila   She doesn't sleep. I can hear her screaming and weeping. But what is she to do? Sleeping in the same bed as she did with Raj. She smells him . . . sees him.

Nitin   My poor, dear friend whom I loved with all my heart died a year ago. Bhabi will never be consoled. I miss him . . . and sometimes I blame myself . . .

Leila   No! He was weak – he couldn't save himself. And you, Babloo, put your own life at risk to save him. Darling boy! (*She caresses his face.*) You've been such a lifeline to us. Helping in the shop. And I am thankful, Babloo . . .

Nitin   I should have died instead! At least nobody would have cared. But now you and Bhabi are bereaved. Why did we go on that boat? I don't want to speak out of turn, but . . .

He looks at the **Doctor** *for approval.*

Doctor   Speak, boy!

Nitin   We all have to decide what is the best thing for Bhabi. She is the important one now. Don't you agree?

Doctor   Yes. What do you suggest?

Nitin   Mother – do I have your permission?

Leila   Please – I am desperate for her . . .

Nitin   She needs a constant companion. A woman of her age has to have the support of a man. A husband is what she needs.

Leila   How can we possibly do that?

Nitin *knows that he has them in his grasp. He suddenly changes the tone by breaking out of the conversation, leaving his suggestion floating in the air.*

Nitin   May I talk to her?

Leila   Tell her to come out of her misery.

Nitin   I will give her a few words of comfort. That is all that I can do . . .

He goes, leaving **Leila** *and the* **Doctor**.

Doctor   As you say, Leila, it's a desperate situation. And quite possibly, as time goes on, she may get worse, and there is the likelihood that . . .

Leila   What?

Doctor   Well . . . She may lose her grasp on reality . . .

The **Doctor** *and* **Leila** *mull things over.* **Nitin** *is in* **Rani**'s *room.* **Nitin** *sees* **Rani** *staring at him. He grabs her and shakes her.*

Nitin   Pull yourself together!

Rani   I can't sleep – I see him . . .

Nitin   So do I. I can't even walk up the stairs to my room at night. Every creak, every gust of wind sends shudders down my spine. We've spent a year apart. Now I want to spend the nights with you.

Rani   I see him so clearly . . .

Nitin   I spent last night under a bridge watching the flowing river. I couldn't face my room. I see things – that night on the river in Kullu Valley . . .

The sounds of fireworks.

Nitin   The fireworks . . . as if it were happening now. But we must, we must imagine that his death was natural. He was dealt a bad hand by fortune and this has allowed us to be together. You do know that we can never be with anybody else? We did what we did because we want to be together . . .

Rani   Yes . . .

Nitin   Then let's be together. Marry me. They have the idea in their heads now . . .

She moves nearer to him. They embrace.

Nitin   Play your part, my angel. Show them what they want to see. Come with me.

Nitin *follows* **Rani** *into the lounge where the* **Doctor** *and* **Leila** *are as before.*

Rani   I just want to sleep forever. Never wake up. I want to be with Raj . . .

Leila   Please child. Drink some tea, Rani. You'll feel better . . .

Doctor   I have been seeing what has been happening in this house and it's not good, Leila. Not for you, nor for the girl. And what Nitin said is the right way forward. The more I think about it, the more I hate myself for not thinking of this solution earlier.

Nitin   I think myself a part of the family and therefore have a duty to do what is best for you, Mother, and for Bhabi. I didn't mean to offend you, Bhabi . . .

Nitin *discreetly signals to her. She suddenly starts to sob and walks into a corner of the room staring at the wall.*

Doctor   Leila, you owe it to Rani and most importantly, the memory of your son, that she is cared for . . .

Leila   Can't you see the fear in her eyes? Every moment is torture. The world has been cruel to her . . .

Doctor   Precisely. Therefore, a new reason to live is what she needs.

Leila   I could never introduce a stranger into this house. That would kill her. She still loves my son. Raj is forever in her memory. She puts fresh flowers around his picture every day . . .

Nitin *nods his head to* **Rani**, *discreetly.* **Rani** *walks out of the room.*

Doctor   Leila – sometimes God manipulates things in strange ways. He throws difficulties at us, but always provides a way out of those hardships. And Nitin is right. In my opinion, the perfect companion for her is in our midst.

The **Doctor** *looks at* **Nitin**. **Nitin** *feigns surprise.*

Nitin   But, Doctor . . . How could you think that?

Leila   But he was Raj's closest friend . . .

Doctor   Exactly! Think about it. Where else would you find a better husband than Nitin? A friend of the family, a trustworthy, genuine man. You love him don't you?

Leila *walks over to* **Nitin** *and strokes his head.*

Leila   And Rani and Nitin have always been like brother and sister . . .

Doctor   You will have somebody to look after you and as you said, we don't want a stranger in the house at all. Nitin is a bull of a man, capable of giving Rani many children. What do you think, Nitin?

Nitin   I am not worthy of this family. I am just a meandering artist. What can I possibly give to Bhabi?

Leila *starts to weep. She finds solace on the* **Doctor**'s *shoulders.*

Leila   How can I think of another man giving Rani what my son didn't . . .

Doctor   You know how I feel about destiny and star charts? Let's consult my oracle . . .

He fiddles through his bag to find what he wants. He brings out a huge chart. He dons his glasses and suddenly acts very official, as if he is doing something very important.

Doctor   Nitin – please write down your date of birth, place of birth and the time of birth. Also, I need your father's date of birth and the village or city in which he was born.

Nitin *writes this down, whilst the* **Doctor** *flicks through his charts. He reads* **Nitin***'s writing and concentrates on the chart, whilst* **Nitin** *and* **Leila** *wait for him to come to a conclusion.*

Leila   I didn't even offer you some tea. I'll get it . . .

Nitin   No, Mother. Just some water.

Leila *pours some water from a nearby jug and hands it to* **Nitin***.*

Doctor   Now. That is Rani's chart . . . and that is Nitin's.

He gets a big magnifying glass out and tries to work out some calculations.

Doctor   Ahhhhhh! Believe it or not, Nitin's chart is very similar to Raj's. The difference being in the lifeline length. You see, there . . . a match? Is that enough to convince you? It's also a fact that the dark star is nowhere to be seen. That suggests a close to hundred per cent chance of success. Life is about chances. This is another chance for you, Leila, and for Rani . . .

The **Doctor** *and* **Leila** *talk as if* **Nitin** *is not there.* **Nitin** *knows the best thing to do is listen. Things are going his way. He fiddles with the charts and strolls to a corner of the room, pouring himself some water.*

Leila   Why would he marry a widow – Nitin?

Nitin   I only have you Mother, and Bhabi. And if I were to gain a family, then I would be the happiest man alive.

Doctor   Leila, they both love you. They want you to be happy. There is no reason why we should not do the roka ceremony this evening. Why not? Nitin is not a philanderer. Call Rani – let's talk to her. Rani!

Leila   You know that I respect your opinion.

Doctor   I have seen Rani and Nitin – everybody is unhappy and it should stop. The mourning needs to stop.

Rani *enters.*

Rani   Yes?

Leila   The Doctor has something to say.

Doctor   We feel that this sadness has gone on long enough.

Rani   I am still grieving for my husband. It will take a long time to forget him.

Doctor   I know, beti, but – you must think of your mother. She is not well. Seeing you like this makes her weep. Your husband is dead. You have your whole life ahead of you . . .

Rani   What do you want?

Leila   For us to live as we used to live. We won't have Raj, but he will be amongst us and we will always think of him. The love that you had for him and that I had for him will never die. He was my Krishna . . .

Doctor   We feel that you should remarry.

Rani   No! I can never do that to the memory of my husband. Nobody could ever take his place.

Doctor   Nitin is a good man . . .

Leila   Nitin is already a part of the family and he needs us. Who else has he got?

Rani   I do want to make you happy, Mother . . .

Leila   It will be difficult, but slowly we will learn to live again . . . My darling boy . . .

Nitin   Mother.

He touches her feet.

Rani   I love Nitin like a brother.

Nitin   And I love Rani as a sister.

Leila   You have a duty, Nitin. You can see that?

Nitin   Yes . . .

Rani   I wanted to cry in peace – to be left alone in grief . . .

Leila   We are altogether in this. Am I being selfish, Doctor Sahib?

Doctor   No.

Leila   An old woman being stupid and scared at the thought of being left alone in her old age . . .

Nitin   Why would you be left alone? We are here . . .

Doctor   Maybe we should leave them alone to talk?

Nitin *looks at* **Rani**. *A long gaze.*

Nitin   There is nothing to talk about.

Rani   No.

Nitin   I understand what you want – Rani?

Rani *stares at him and nods in agreement.*

Nitin   We are your children and we want to make you happy. Rani – do you agree?

Rani   Yes.

The **Doctor** *urges her to unite the pair's hands.* **Leila** *takes* **Rani***'s hand and puts it into* **Nitin***'s.* **Leila** *takes her shawl off and throws it over the both of them (the traditional ceremony when a brother takes on a dead brother's wife). She adjusts the shawl over their shoulders.*

Leila   The ceremony of the dirty sheet will take place when the brother of the dead husband takes the wife to be his own. I will give the two of you all that I have: the savings, the deeds to the shop, everything. I give myself to your kindness. We will be secure and live happily. Don't look so sad, children. This is the new beginning. May you be the mother of a thousand sons . . .

Nitin   We will love and care for you, Mother.

Leila *sobs violently and falls to the floor. The* **Doctor** *consoles her. The two, hands held, stare.*

Scene Two

The bedroom. **Rani** *walks in, as if treading each step carefully.* **Nitin** *studies her. He is fully dressed in wedding gear and a glittery veil hangs over his face. He takes his wedding coat off and moves nearer to her. As he is about to put his hand to her face she shrugs him off.*

Rani   Don't – please . . .

Nitin   It's all right. We have arrived where we wanted to be safely. Don't fret, little angel.

Rani   Don't speak to me like that!

Nitin *looks at her for a few moments. She looks around the room.*

Rani   This room has been like a prison. Where I was captured since I was a child.

Nitin   Then we shall move to another place . . .

Rani   Where? Where will you take me?

Nitin   Why are you so angry? A year is enough to get over it . . .

Rani   Look at your neck – that's where he bit you . . .

Nitin   We are alone and free. Free to do as we want. Laugh out loud. They want to hear us be happy . . .

Rani   Die. That's all I want – but death won't come to me . . .

Nitin   I am not putting up with this – you are my wife! Hold me . . .

He grabs her arms as if to put them around him.

Nitin   Just embrace me. Hold me and it will all be all right . . .

Rani's *arms just hang by her side.*

Rani   I might as well have killed myself as well.

Nitin   Come on, Rani. Let's just think of what we have had – how much you wanted me? Don't you want me now?

Rani   Her poor boy – drowned . . .

Nitin   Have you forgotten our secret meetings when I used to come and see you? We can rekindle that love and desire. I will stay the whole night with you. And you will find me in the morning in your bosom. Isn't that what you want? It's just you and me now. There is no Raj . . .

Rani   Don't. I don't want to hear his name.

Awkward pause.

Nitin   The flowers are nice.

She studies the vase uncomfortably.

Rani   She needn't have spent all that money.

Nitin   She is happy.

Rani   Yes – are you happy?

Nitin   Yes – now that I have you . . .

The clear figure of **Raj** *is seen, struggling as he did. His big, dead eyes stare accusatorily at the couple. He points at* **Nitin**.

Nitin   There is no more Raj . . .

The figure starts smiling.

Nitin   There is no more Raj!

He repeats this loudly and attacks the figure. The figure disappears.

Nitin   He is no more. You are mine. The past is the past. He died by accident. It was an accident . . .

Rani   Did you see him, after? Did you go with Mother? Did you see him? When they found him?

Nitin   Yes . . .

Rani   What did he look like?

Nitin   What do you want me to say? I saw his body – all right? And he was nothing but a sack of bones and decomposing meat . . .

Rani (*shudders at the thought*)   Meat – that's all he was?

Nitin   It's cold here. As if . . . Hold my hand. Let's warm each other. I haven't held you for a year . . .

Rani   Don't touch me.

They stand apart, staring at each other. A slight knocking sound.

Nitin   What's that?

Rani   I don't know – go and see . . .

Nitin   No.

Rani   It's a scraping on the window.

Nitin   It's him – haunting us. Go and have a look . . .

Rani *walks towards the window, slowly.*

Rani   It's Hanuman – the monkey. Look, he's staring at us . . .

Nitin *goes closer to the window.*

Nitin   It's Raj. Maybe his soul has taken over the monkey's – these things happen. They say that we have eight million and four hundred thousand lives before we are born. Maybe his spirit has travelled into the monkey.

Rani   Are you mad, or are you joking?

Nitin   Look at his eyes . . . as if he knows everything . . .

Rani   No . . .

Rani *picks up a stick and shoos the monkey away.*

Rani   Go! Go!

Nitin   We must be strong. Nothing can get in our way except ourselves. We can't fail now! Try and look in your mind's eye. See us as we were. The passion. The lust. Let's sleep now. Our wedding bed is ready . . .

Rani   I can't. Let's just talk . . .

Nitin   About what?

Rani   Anything . . .

Nitin   All right. They might give me a new job – move me up. But I am thinking about giving up the job altogether and studying my art . . .

Rani   Now that you have a ready-made bank of money?

Nitin   She is giving that to us because she wants to. I didn't ask her for it – it is your dowry . . .

Rani   But it's all very convenient for you, isn't it? A big place to live in. A wife, a rich mother leaving all her fortune to you . . .

Nitin   To us. You think that that is all I want?

Rani   Yes.

Nitin   What demon has possessed you? Kiss me . . .

Rani   I can't.

Nitin   Just hold me and everything will be all right . . .

He goes closer to her and touches her head as if to kiss her.

Nitin   Kiss me like you used to . . .

Rani   No.

Nitin   They want to hear us laugh. The badness has gone – kiss me . . .

Rani   No.

He grabs her by the neck and forces her mouth to meet his. A savage kiss. She won't respond. He gets up.

Nitin   Damned woman! Do what you want. I am going to sleep.

Darkness. **Rani** *is staring into nothingness.* **Nitin** *sits on the bed.*

Rani   Forgive me, Raj. Forgive me . . . I will do anything to repent. I wish I had never met him. Please forgive me . . .

She starts uttering prayers.

Nitin   Come to bed with me. Are you afraid that your dead Raj will come to torment you?

Rani   He is already here, Nitin. Haunting both you and me . . .

Nitin   Am I married to you and his ghost now? Is that what you want? We'll go insane . . .

They stare at each other wondering what to do.

Scene Three

The lounge. **Leila** *sits on a chair. She has a blanket around her.*

Doctor   My turn to be your servant . . .

Leila   So quickly old age has come upon me . . .

Doctor   You have your children to look after you now. She's weak. Make sure she eats properly. It's just a minor infection.

Leila   Nitin – you know that you have everything now – you and Rani . . .

Nitin   All we want is for you to get better. So will you?

Leila   Yes. I'll try . . .

Doctor   Rani will look after the house and I'll organise for a servant boy to come later today.

Nitin   Mother – I have made a decision today. I feel that I need to start being an artist again . . .

Rani *stares at him.*

Nitin   I have given my notice.

Rani   What? How could you? Who will pay for the house? The shop? You will be depending on me for money. On me and Mother . . .

Nitin   Don't you think that I have thought this out?

Rani   Yes. Only too well . . .

Nitin   I want to hire a studio and paint all day . . .

Rani   And who will pay for that?

Leila   Beti – he has deserved it. After looking after you and me. Let him find a small room to do his work.

Nitin   The interest from the investment that Mother has given us will pay for everything that I need including an expenses fund. I have talked it over with the lawyers today and with Mother's blessings and your consent, Rani, I can get on with what I need . . .

Leila   The money is there for you and your wife. The Doctor will help you to arrange the monthly payments from the bank and you can have a . . .

She starts to whine, as if crying. Her mouth remains open and she starts frothing at the mouth.

Rani   What's happened?

The **Doctor** *studies* **Leila** *closely. He holds her mouth. He takes out a torch and shines it in her eyes.*

Doctor   Can you hear me Leila? (*He continues to study her pulse, etc.*)

Rani   Mother – are you in pain? Why is she looking at us like that? There is no life in her eyes. Like a child. What's happened?

Doctor   Leila – can you hear me? Listen to me. (*Aside to* **Rani** *and* **Nitin**.) Don't panic too much. Looks like she has suffered a stroke. Try to remain calm in front of her. We don't want to make things worse. We need to get her to a hospital urgently. Hasn't Ishfaq from across the way got a van?

Rani   Yes . . . cold . . .

She feels **Leila**'s *feet.*

Rani   Mother?

She holds her.

Rani   Please don't leave us – we need you. How will I live now on my own? How will we cope?

Scene Four

The bedroom. **Nitin** *and* **Rani** *are fighting. She pulls his hair and he beats her.*

Nitin   We can't behave like this, Rani. Please . . . we can't be victims any more. Let's take control – together. We are in love . . .

Rani   No! I don't feel anything for you. . .

Nitin   Yes, you do. You want me. Hold me and we can face anything . . . We have been married a few months and soon we can move. Leave this town – leave it all behind . . .

Rani   Can we?

Nitin   Yes. We will go back to the country, to the open air . . . where you can see the mountains . . . where you can see the colourful birds . . . like you did when you were a child.

Rani   Yes – that is what I would like . . .

Nitin   So we must be calm. Don't let these nights be a living hell.

Rani   I want to bite out your neck. I want to create a deeper wound.

The night falls. They lie in bed. Silence. A pause. **Nitin** *turns to put his hand over* **Rani**. **Raj**'s *figure gets up.* **Nitin** *screams in terror, almost on the verge of tears.*

Nitin   Save me . . .

Nitin *takes her in his arms. They could almost be fighting.*

Nitin   You will find rest in my arms . . .

She bites his neck. **Nitin** *cries out in agony.*

Nitin   NO! Please . . .

Nitin *throws her to the floor, still smarting from the attack.*
Nitin *then sits astride her and holds her, on the verge of tears.*

Nitin   Only you can save me and only I can save you. Will you be my saviour – please?

Nitin *takes her violently. She is screaming in terror.*

Nitin   I will drive the ghosts out of our lives. We will finish him for good . . .

Raj *is watching him. He laughs.*

Nitin   I will drive you out!

They sit staring into the darkness. They haven't won the battle yet.

Act Four

Scene One

The lounge – a few weeks later. **Nitin** *carries* **Leila** *in and puts her in her chair.* **Rani** *enters carrying* **Leila***'s blankets, which she puts on her chair.* **Leila** *stares into the distance, occasionally blinking.*

Rani   Today is Thursday, Mother. The Doctor will be coming round. Here – take your fish oil . . .

She puts the tablets in **Leila***'s mouth and holds a glass of water to her mouth.* **Nitin** *and* **Rani** *stand awkwardly, focusing their energies on* **Leila***.*

Nitin   Don't look at me like that – like I am a dog. . .

Rani   Please, Nitin . . . (*Indicating* **Leila**.)

Nitin   What about her? She can't hear . . .

Rani   She can hear everything.

Nitin   I have found a studio. I went there today. I had forgotten what art was like – forgotten everything because a woman misled me! I should have just continued my free and debauched life . . .

Rani   You can do what you want. Leave now . . . leave! See – you won't. Who would pay for you if you left? You'd have to work – something that you are incapable of . . .

Nitin   Why do you go on and on about money? Is that all you think I wanted? Is it?

A knocking.

Nitin   He is here.

Rani *exits to open the door.* **Nitin** *stares at* **Leila** *piteously.*

Doctor   How is she?

Nitin   The same.

Doctor   Well her complexion looks healthy. Can she swallow food all right?

Rani   She takes in most of it, but I've been giving her liquids . . .

Doctor   Good. As long as she is kept healthy. Now – shall we have a game of karom, Nitin?

Nitin   I don't feel like it somehow . . .

Rani   I will play.

Doctor   Look at her – like an innocent child . . . Are you well, Leila?

He stares at her.

Doctor   Yes – she's happy. To be looked after by such devoted children. Why don't you move her chair closer to the window? Get a bit of light on her face . . .

Nitin   She's fine as she is.

Doctor   I think a bit of light is what she needs – don't you?

Leila – *frozen.*

Doctor   See? Did you see her flicker her finger? She wants to be near the window. Knowing somebody for so long enables you to understand their every expression . . .

Nitin *begrudgingly moves* **Leila**'*s chair.* **Leila** *swings involuntarily, highlighting her complete dependence on* **Nitin** *and* **Rani**.

Doctor   Carefully, yaar . . . I think that she is happy. She always wanted to know that she would be cared for in her old age. You know what you should do? That painting that you cleverly made of Raj – where is it?

Nitin   Somewhere . . .

Doctor   Hidden away? No – put it up so that she can see it. It will keep her soul happy.

Nitin   No, Doctor. I think I am capable of keeping my own house in order, as I see fit . . .

Rani   Nitin . . .

Nitin   I don't think it will do her any good to be reminded of exactly what we have all been trying to forget for the last year and a half.

Doctor   As you wish. Anyway – I must go. Can't keep the old patients waiting.

Exit, visibly hurt.

Rani   You insulted him!

Nitin   He's an interfering fool! What business is it of his what I hang up on my wall? In my house?

Rani   Your house?

Nitin   Yes – I am the man of the house . . .

Rani   A man reliant on the income of an old woman's money?

Nitin   Stop prattling. My head is spinning around – all the things I have to do, should have done . . . I am young and what have I done? Just thrown it all away. Why don't you feed her? Look at her – she looks pathetic . . .

Rani   Don't – if you must shout, then do it in the bedroom.

Nitin   No! Are you afraid now?

Rani   Yes . . .

Nitin   Of what?

Rani   Ghosts . . .

Nitin   Well, we are surrounded by them – ghosts . . .

He sobs in agony and fear.

Rani   How will I find peace?

Nitin   You won't now. Neither will I. Why don't we torture ourselves further – let's take pain and angst to the extreme. Wait . . .

He exits. She stares at **Leila***.*

Rani   I am sorry, Mother . . . sorry for everything . . .

A sudden vision of **Raj** *being cradled by* **Leila** *in her lap.* **Rani** *looks again and the ghost has disappeared.*

Nitin *comes in, carrying the painting of* **Raj***. He looks like a man possessed.*

Nitin   Maybe the Doctor was right. We should put this in this room, in front of everybody . . .

He puts it in front of **Leila***.*

Nitin   Look. Yellow flesh, receding hair, exactly like . . . when . . .

Rani   No! No . . . Mother – I will feed you now.

Nitin   Looking like his dead self even when he was alive.

Rani   He's just talking nonsense . . .

Nitin   A walking dead man. Look at him in this painting, old woman . . .

Rani   Nitin! You are not well. Please . . .

Nitin   He looked like that. My head is hurting – why won't it go away? Why is my body aging so quickly? This last year I have become a frail old man, unable to deal with life. My head . . .

He beats his head violently.

Nitin   Go away pain! Go! Go!

Rani   No!

Nitin *forces the picture into* **Rani***'s face. He holds her throat with one hand.*

Nitin   Yes – look at the picture! Look! Ahhhhh! He looked like that . . . when we killed him!

Leila *suddenly shrieks and resumes her frozen state.*

Rani   What have you done? You animal!

Nitin   Look at her eyes – full of hatred. She wants to kill me. Look! You want to look at me, old woman? Well go on then . . .

He stares at her face.

Nitin   Look all you want. Your hate won't kill me. I'm hungry . . .

Rani   What do you want me to do about it?

Nitin   Can't you feed me properly?

Rani   If you are not happy, then go somewhere else . . .

Nitin   The house is like a pigsty. Don't you clean up any more?

Rani   You have two big fat arms – you do it! Since you took on Mother's money, you have turned into a fatty. All you do is eat, eat . . . Try doing some work! Why are you taking it out on me? You have to live with the guilt – so be a man. Live with it!

Nitin   We are both in it together. We both murdered him . . .

Rani   You did it! You pushed him into the water . . .

Nitin   And you were sitting there, in the boat, urging me to do it! You are as guilty as I am – more guilty, because you betrayed your own husband . . . your own mother . . . You are evil! Evil demon! Say that you accept your guilt . . . say it!

Rani   No – I won't, because it was you and you alone, with your talk of new beginnings . . . and what did you call it? Ghostdancing – freeing your self? Well, this is where your ghostdancing has led us! You are a coward – a whimpering dog. Face the truth: *you* are the murderer! I have no blame attached to my name . . .

Nitin (**Nitin** *holds her and beats her around the head*) When I didn't know you, I was pure – a normal man, living my dull existence in the Railways. Stupidity led me to your door . . . to your flesh . . . your hair . . . I was killed by your beauty. Why did you do that to me?

Rani You did it yourself . . . to yourself! You could have told me that I was being stupid. You could have saved me from myself. Why didn't you talk sense into me? Instead you took my hand and led me to the edge, so I could throw myself in . . .

Rani *turns to* **Leila** *and kneels at her feet.*

Rani It was not me, Mother. He did it. He killed your son. My husband. I was as much a victim as Raj, or you. And he took me in in his terrible scheme. Will you ever understand? Will you forgive me?

Leila *looks grief-stricken. Her lips tremble. She spits.*

Rani Yes? You forgive me? Yes? Oh Mother . . .

She holds her.

Nitin What are you doing? She hates you. She hates us . . .

Rani I am trying to seek forgiveness. And if you did the same, then maybe there would be a chance for you as well . . .

Nitin There is no recourse. No way back.

Rani Why did we do it?

Nitin Ahhhh – you admit your hand in the deed . . .

Rani He was a good man. He wouldn't have hurt anybody . . .

Nitin   He was an imbecile. Incompetent little chicken.
That is what he looked like – a chicken that is about to have
its head twisted off. It's easy to say now what a man he was.
He couldn't have given you what I gave you. I woke you up
from your slumber. I turned you from a girl into a
woman . . .

Rani   I loved him . . .

Nitin   No you didn't. Because if you did, you wouldn't
have let me take you in your bedroom – all those afternoons
when he was out, and she was downstairs . . . and every
opportunity that we had . . . even when they were in the
room. You touched every part of me – why, because you
loved him?

Rani   He may have been less manly than most men, but
he was kind . . .

Nitin   I don't want to hear any more!

Rani   You are surrounded by him – can't you see? The
bed that you sleep in, the house that you live in – everything
is his. And you are a usurper. An imposter . . .

Nitin   You don't realise what you are doing . . .

Rani   He showed his love, yes, because we were so used to
each other's presence, it was as if we were one . . .

Nitin   I don't want to hear any more about him.

*He grabs her by the neck, as if strangling her. He brings her down to
the floor and proceeds to kick her.*

Nitin   Understand? No more! We are doomed. We can't
go anywhere, because that will be sure proof. Then they'll
find us, and . . .

Rani   Burn our heads in oil!

*He slaps her and she slaps him back, harder.
A knocking.*

Nitin   What is that? The police! They've come to get us –
they're here! Have you told them? Did you go and give it all
away?

Rani   No . . .

Nitin   How do I know? You go out a lot – who do you talk
to?

Rani   Nobody . . .

Nitin   Who do you talk to? Where do you go?

Knocking.

Nitin   Answer it. It's the Law come to get me . . .

Rani   No – it's not . . .

Nitin   Who is it then?

Rani   Hanuman . . .

Nitin   The monkey . . .

Rani   He's running up and down all the walls of the house
now, as if he's going mad . . .

Nitin   He wants the murderers dead!

Rani   It's just a monkey . . .

Nitin   I told you he was possessed. I've tried to ignore it,
but even when I go to the studio to do some thinking and
some work, I can see it following me. . .

Rani   Stupid fool! A monkey following you?

Nitin *rushes to the window.*

Nitin   Don't you see who it is? It's him! Look at its eyes
. . . bloodshot . . .

Rani   I'm not wasting time thinking about monkeys . . .

Nitin   Why? You've got better things to do, have you?
Old women to look after, shops that have no customers
because there is nobody to serve them . . .

Rani   Go and kill it then . . . If you are so manly – kill it!

Nitin *runs out. Sounds of the monkey screaming to death.* **Nitin**'s *shadowy figure is seen twisting its neck.*

Scene Two

Nitin *is in the lounge.* **Leila** *is in her chair.* **Nitin** *has the dead monkey laid out. He is copying the monkey's shape on to a canvas. He is whistling as he does this.*

Nitin   Are you hungry, Mother?

He waits for a response which he knows he will never get.

Nitin   No? Well, it's just as well – she is not here and I can't cook. Shall I tell you something, Mother? I followed her today. I was afraid that she would go to the police station. But you would be happy, wouldn't you – if that is what she did? I followed her. She was wearing a flowing sari and she had put on her face the kind of make-up that foreign women wear . . . and she knew that every man on the street was looking at her. That is what she wanted . . . And do you know where she went? D'Souza Marg – where I had my bachelor home, remember? And I saw her hold the arm of a young man – he had a small moustache and a golden watch. He took her on his arm and they went into a lodging house. I thought I saw her through the window, with the man's hand on her breasts . . . I'm happy actually – you might not believe me, but I am happy. At least she's occupying herself. So I shall start doing the same thing myself – getting on with my life . . .

He continues painting. The door sounds.

Nitin   Aren't you coming in? It's dinnertime and there is no food . . .

Rani (*off*)   What do you want me to do about it?

Nitin   Come in here . . .

Rani (*off*)   I want to have a wash!

Nitin   Come here . . . Now!

Rani wanders in. Her clothes are awry – hair is a mess and she is slightly drunk.

Nitin   Look at you – you stink!

Rani   I told you – I want to wash . . .

Nitin   You can't ignore me like this. I need food, she needs to be fed . . . and who do you think is going to do it? Look at you – a proper slut! Come here . . .

He grabs her.

Rani   Leave me alone . . .

Nitin   I want some money. I have decided to get on with my life, as you are clearly getting on with yours. I want fifty thousand rupees . . .

Rani   What for? So that you can squander everything that I have? No . . .

Nitin   Fifty thousand . . .

Rani   The shop is finished – nobody buys anymore . . .

Nitin   Well, if you were there serving people, instead of . . . finding new friends, then maybe it would have a chance . . .

Rani   You are not getting any more from me.

Nitin   Tell the bank that you have authorised the withdrawal, otherwise they won't give me anything . . .

Rani   Aren't you listening? We are heading for disaster. There is no income, just the savings . . . If you want to go back to where you came from . . .

Nitin   What – D'Souza Marg?

Rani (*as if she hasn't heard him*) . . . then you are welcome to do so. I have to look after myself. I won't have you living at my expense anymore. It's finished . . .

Nitin   I want that money. I need my peace of mind and it will allow me to buy instruments for my art . . .

Rani *looks at the pathetic image of the monkey and the canvas.*

Nitin   And you can do what you want . . .

Rani   You won't get anything more from me. I won't authorise anything. And if you go and try, they won't let you. The Doctor saw to it that you couldn't possibly go running off with Mother's fortune . . .

Nitin *looks as if he is about to hit her.*

Nitin   All right . . . Well, there is no other way then. I am going mad . . . I can't live with myself any longer . . . We are both going to confess everything – that way, it will all be finished with . . .

Rani   Are you trying to scare me? If that is what you want to do, then let's do it. Come on . . . let's go to the thana and speak to the Superintendent . . .

They are about to go. **Rani** *panics.*

Rani   All right – I'll authorise the money. Happy? Now I need a wash . . .

Nitin *resumes painting.*

Blackout.

Scene Three

A month later. **Nitin**, *looking as if he hasn't slept for days, stares at the painting of the monkey and the painting of* **Raj***, facing each other like a ridiculous display.* **Rani** *is staring into oblivion.* **Leila** *watches over them.* **Nitin** *takes her arm. He starts to weep.*

Nitin   We are imprisoned . . .

Rani   Yes.

Nitin   I have been around the town, spending her money
. . . drinking . . . whoring . . . trying to get back what I had.
It's gone forever. Whenever I am out with a woman it
makes everything even worse . . .

Rani   There is no escape. We are tied by a bond – a blood
bond. You won't tell anybody about anything, will you?

Nitin   No. We should act as if nothing has happened. Is
that so difficult? But I don't trust you. And look at her – she
is smiling . . .

Rani   I know that you have been following me. Whenever
I go out, you are there . . .

Nitin   I want some whisky. Get it for me . . .

She goes out. **Leila** *stares.* **Nitin** *gets out a bottle from his coat.*

Nitin   Suspicion – that is what I live with all day and night
. . . What will she do? Who will she tell?

Rani *returns. She is hiding a knife in her clothing, which she holds
with one hand. She puts the whisky and water on a table.*

Nitin   We will go to bed. I want you to have some whisky
with me . . .

Rani   No.

Nitin   Why? You drink with those prostitutes – why can't
you have a glass with me?

Rani *turns around. She prepares the knife. She approaches* **Nitin**
who is pouring the whisky. He adds some liquid from the phial.

Nitin   It's something new – try it. What is that?

Rani   What?

Nitin   In your hands . . .

Rani *takes out the knife. She weeps.*

Nitin What are you planning to do with that? Kill me?

He laughs, which builds up to a fit of hysterics.

Rani Hold me – I'm scared . . .

Nitin *holds her.*

Nitin So you were planning to kill me? Funny that – because I was planning to kill you. Yes . . . yes . . .

He holds the phial of poison up in the air.

Nitin I stole poison from the Doctor. We are at the end of the road . . .

They share a glance – a slight smile – because the end of the pain is near. She plunges the knife into him a few times.

Nitin Ahhhh!

Rani We are finished . . . Give me the drink . . .

She fumbles for the phial and drinks the poison. She drops to the floor.

Nitin I will be my own judge and prosecutor. This will finish me off . . .

He stumbles, taking the phial of poison from her hand, and drinks it.

Nitin The spectacle is over . . .

Nitin *and* **Rani** *writhe in agony, dying. The paintings watch over them.* **Leila** *suddenly jumps up and screams in triumph like a banshee.*

Leila *(barely able to breathe)* The murderers are dead . . .

She falls on the chair. She could be dead. There is a knocking. We hear the last breaths of the murderers. Louder knocking.

Doctor Where is everybody? Can somebody open . . . I have the police with me . . . There are allegations . . . We have to get to the bottom of all this . . .

The knocking continues.

Blackout.